ROBERT L THOMPSON

TVA ARCHITECTS

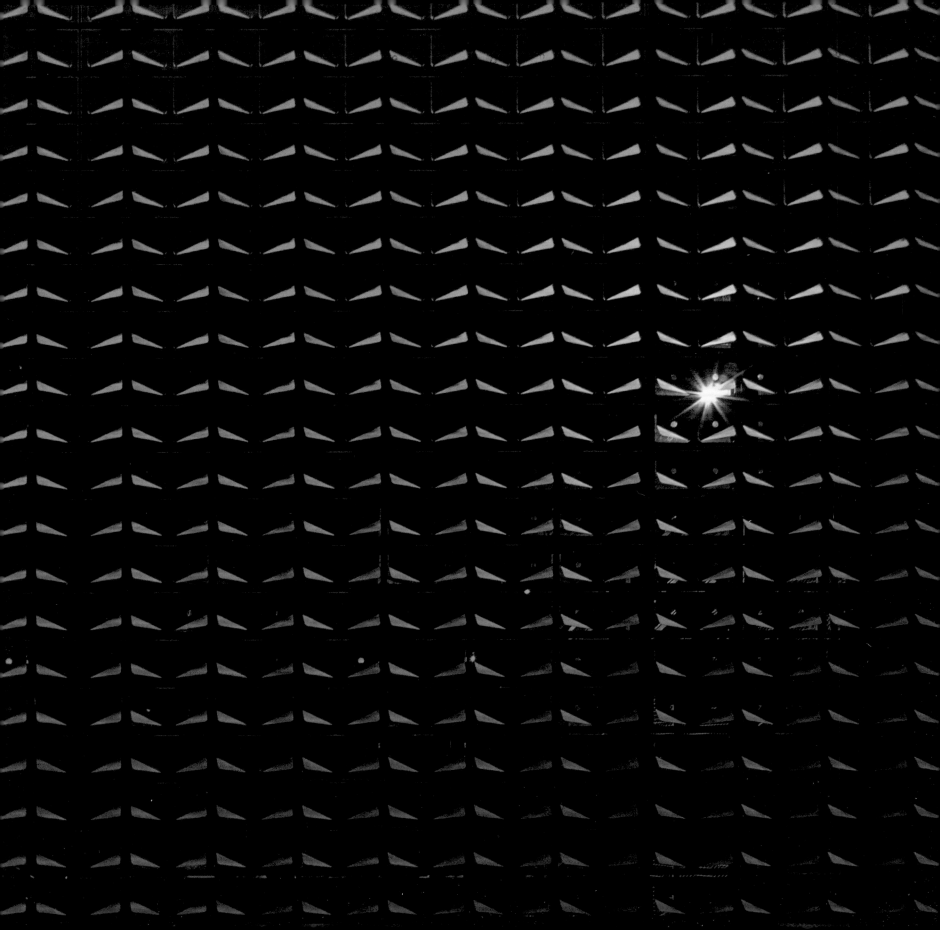

ROBERT L THOMPSON

TVA ARCHITECTS

INTRODUCTION BY RANDY GRAGG

FOREWORD BY MICHAEL J. CROSBIE

images
Publishing

CONTENTS

8   **PREFACE**
    Robert L. Thompson

10 **THE AGILE ARCHITECT**
    Randy Gragg

16 **AN ARCHITECTURE OF BALANCE**
    Michael J. Crosbie

WORKPLACE, CORPORATE & COMMERCIAL

20   Ford Alumni Center
30   Banfield Corporate Headquarters
44   GSA / SSA Call Center
52   Metro Headquarters
60   Murphy Corporate Offices
72   Nike Asian Corporate Headquarters
86   Sony Ericsson Headquarters
98   Park Avenue West Tower
108 Fox Tower
118 Vancouver Office Tower
124 Ochoco Air Hangar
138 Nike Air Hangar
146 Fort Dalles Training Center
156 Nike Retail Stores

ARTS, SPORTS & CULTURE

- 184 SOU Performing Arts Center
- 194 Moyer Mausoleum
- 200 Ankeny Plaza Pavilion
- 206 Director Park Pavilions
- 214 Matthew Knight Arena
- 230 Coaches Office MKA
- 240 Nike World Headquarters
- 264 Bo Jackson Fitness Center
- 272 Nolan Ryan Building
- 284 Jerry Rice Building
- 292 Nike Gatehouse
- 298 The Park
- 302 Mia Hamm Design Center
- 314 Tiger Woods Conference Center
- 322 Nike Sports Performance Center

RESIDENTIAL, HOUSING & HOSPITALITY

- 334 Alden/Drummond Residence
- 342 Crabbe Residence
- 352 Frankel Residence
- 362 Fritz Residence
- 374 West Hills Residence
- 384 Pearl Apartments
- 390 John Ross Tower
- 400 Goose Hollow Lofts
- 408 EVO Tower
- 414 The Aniva Apartments
- 420 The Caring Cabin
- 428 Greve Residence
- 436 Vancouver Waterfront Condominium Tower
- 442 Alder 9 Apartments

APPENDIX

- 448 Biography
- 450 TVA Employees & Collaborators
- 452 Selected Publications
- 454 Awards & Contributions
- 456 Project Credits
- 462 Acknowledgments

PREFACE

ROBERT L. THOMPSON

It has been both humbling and rewarding to look back across my collected body of work spanning nearly 40 years. Every project brings back a wealth of memories reliving the journey I have taken throughout the evolution of each of them. The life experience one shares with clients, collaborators, and builders throughout the process of creating architecture has enriched my life to no end.

One of the challenges has been deciding which projects to include that best captures the diversity in scale, complexity, and typology that best represents one's evolution as a designer and architect across four decades of work. I have carefully selected 43 projects that are encompassed in this collection of work that attempt to tell that story. Each one of these buildings has informed the rest, complementing and contradicting each other at the same time. Although each project continues to further ideas explored in the previous one, every creation addresses a new theme and program unique to its special and specific conditions.

Rather than order the projects chronologically I have presented these select works based on typology. Each project is different in size, type, scale, program, and place illustrating the various approaches and ideas with which I have confronted architecture. What has become evident in my body of work is that throughout my career I have never veered far from my vision and the driving principals around modernism that have guided my work as a designer and an architect. Throughout my life I have had a preoccupation with space related to human scale, to spatial volume, and the interplay of geometric form and light, and its engagement with the personal experience of living in and moving through these spaces.

I founded TVA Architects (Thompson Vaivoda & Associates) in 1984 with then-partners Edward Vaivoda and David Gellos and we spent our first decade designing private office buildings, tech centers as well as housing projects, winning numerous design awards along the way.

In 1987 after three years in practice we won a national design competition to design the Nike World Headquarters, a 12-building 1.1-million-square-foot corporate campus that propelled our firm to the next level specific to project size and complexity.

In the 1990s we experienced exponential growth designing museums, our first high-rise tower as well as a new corporate campus in Dallas, Texas, for Sony Ericsson. Additionally, we doubled the size of the Nike World Headquarters, known as the North Campus expansion, which was honored with nine AIA design awards, in addition to being selected as the International Corporate Campus of the year.

In the first decade of the twenty-first century, our expansion continued with notable new high-rise towers, including the John Ross Tower, the Fox Tower in Portland as well as the EVO Tower in Los Angeles. We completed the critically acclaimed Matthew Knight Arena (a new 12,500-seat basketball arena) and the Ford Alumni Center both on the University of Oregon campus, which opened up new opportunities for us as we expanded the firm's portfolio to include public and institutional works.

The last decade, 2010–2020, has been a period of expansion in terms of building typology and working abroad. As Nike has continued its explosive growth, our work with them has taken us to China where we completed their new 650,000-square-foot Nike Asian Corporate Headquarters in Shanghai in addition to partnering with Nike Retail Design on the rebranding and design of their flagship stores throughout the United States. In 2016 we celebrated the opening of the iconic Park Avenue West Tower in Portland as well as the highly acclaimed Banfield Corporate Headquarters Campus in Vancouver, Washington.

The assemblage of this monograph has brought me back to the realization that our best work is a direct by-product of being blessed with great clients who have shared a deep passion for design, building, and the art of creating significant works of architecture. I am deeply indebted to them for their trust and faith in our work and for the valued relationships that I have developed with them both personally and professionally over the past 40 years. My life as an architect has enabled me to travel extensively throughout Europe, Asia, and the United States working on unique challenging projects, studying architecture and history, researching and experiencing different cultures and ways of life that have had a profound impact on me as a designer throughout my career.

As an architect I am constantly asked, "When you look back over your long career and extensive body of work, what do you consider to be your greatest creation in life?" That's an easy answer for me; it's my children: Barclay, Brooks, and Blake. Nothing can ever compare. They have helped me to understand the past, and have given meaning to my future. They have shown me truth and beauty, and for that I will be forever grateful.

Top left: Kruse Way Plaza, 1984. **Middle left:** Mia Hamm Design Center, Nike World Headquarters, 2000. **Bottom left:** Matthew Knight Arena, 2010. **Right:** Park Avenue West Tower, 2019.

215 NW Park remains a modernist yet refined design showcasing minimalism.

THE AGILE ARCHITECT

RANDY GRAGG

Slotted between two nondescript brick buildings in the last vestiges of Portland's first industrial neighborhood, 215 NW Park still shimmers like the striking alien that landed 40 years ago. A quintet of slender cylindrical steel columns, laterally braced by a central steel "X," hold up the historic heavy-timber frame building behind, its floors sliced away into curvilinear mezzanines. But it's the façade—butted vertical glass divided into 40-foot-wide horizontal bands by aluminum mullions—that became a billboard for minimalist refinement Portland had not seen before.

Designed by Robert Thompson at age 26, 215 NW Park was an investment both financial and architectural. The plans were the first to bear his stamp as a registered architect. "It was a major moment in Portland architecture, even more because it was not a whole building, but a very pure two-dimensional statement of modernism," recalls prominent Portland architect, Thomas Hacker. "There was nothing in Portland as radical at the time. Bob became a very important architect in the region from very early in his career, at least partially based on the beautifully reductive purity of the Park façade."

Indeed, the retrofit is an early example of the four decades of minimalist architecture by Thompson, from the corporate Valhalla of Nike's World Headquarters to the Matthew Knight Arena's shattering break with the University of Oregon's century-plus-old Ivy League tradition to a collection of some 40 residences, all instantly recognizable as Thompson designs. But more than the "look-at-me" statement, it's 215 NW Park's subtleties that anticipate the architect's future work: a thrifty boldness rooted in large gestures finely wrought and an ongoing argument that respect for context can be additive rather than reductive.

"I've never had projects with large budgets. So much of my career has been focused on trying to elevate the mundane, on making something special without a lot." says Thompson.

"Something special without a lot" sums up a lot of architecture in Portland, a city the historian E. Kimbark McColl wryly described as "always looking for first-class passage on a steerage ticket." A.E. Doyle designed the first open-plan library in the country—what its visionary librarian demanded be "a machine for books"—but he lamented the meager budget, even at the building's ribbon-cutting. Pietro Belluschi cannily employed war-surplus aluminum to create his modernist masterpiece, the Equitable Building, giving the pinched lobby its sublimely frugal elegance with little more than neatly arranged rivets. City leaders infamously built Michael Graves's Portland Building for less than the cost of a standard speculative office building.

Not all of Thompson's architecture has arrived on a "steerage-ticket." But his early navigation of tough budgets honed a discipline that matured into an agility practiced across an extraordinarily wide variety of building types and scales.

Thompson acknowledges debts to Yoshio Taniguchi and, more so, to Le Corbusier. Observers see elements of Eero Saarinen, Richard Neutra, Aldo Rossi, and Peter Eisenman and, given Thompson's early fondness for white buildings and vertically slotted cylindrical forms, most often to Mario Botta and Richard Meier. But what might be seen as similarities or, at times, even quotations, of these architects can be like finding the debt Richard Serra owes to Borromini. Thompson describes, and really shapes, his architecture as sculptor and sensualist than academician, peppering his descriptions with more observations of "shifting planes," "spatial layering," and "light and shadow" than theories or historical lineages.

THE AGILE ARCHITECT

The disarming freedom from dogma, but rigorous attention to program, space, and craftsmanship, has inspired a loyal cadre of clients, nearly all private, who enabled him to design the fourth-, sixth-, and eighth-tallest skyscrapers in Portland's core, 44 buildings for Nike, its Nike Asian Corporate Headquarters, and the instantly recognizable homes. Without discounting his talent or work ethic, there has also been a "right-place/right-time" theme to Thompson's career, coupled with a will to turn every challenge into opportunity.

Neither of Thompson's parents were steeped in the arts or architecture. But his mother fanned his early "fixation with art" into early explorations of drawing. His first impressions of architecture happened in the regular course of Portland life with his father. He recalls at age seven being "overwhelmed" by the enormity of the glass walls and the structural muscularity of Memorial Coliseum (SOM 1959). Equally seminal was seeing the powerful verticality in an architectural model for what became arguably Portland's most assertive work of modernism, the Bank of California (Anshen + Allen 1969).

Thompson credits a high-school drawing class taught by instructor David Bakely as the turning point to his architectural career. "It focused beyond mere rendering and, instead, on design and the problem-solving side of drawing." Upon graduation from high school, where he immersed himself in art and design, he quickly enrolled in UO's School of Architecture and Allied Arts (AAA), now the College of Design. His willfulness quickly emerged. "I loved school," he notes, "but I loved the idea of getting out of school even more."

The charismatic Christopher Alexander had cast a long shadow over AAA's pedagogy. As a visiting professor in the mid-1970s, he incubated his notions of a universal "pattern language" in architecture and urbanism. Thompson shrugged them off. "Alexander was obsessed with detail and complexity and overthinking everything," Thompson recalls. "I wanted to learn how to simplify things as much as possible, to make architecture that was clear, understandable, and straightforward." Taking a year out of college to intern in the office of Skidmore, Owings and Merrill, it reinforced Thompson's obsession with modernism. A larger part of his early education took place outside school in travels throughout the United States, Asia, and Europe, studying the work of Richard Meier, Charles Gwathmey, Norman Foster, Tadao Ando, and Alvar Aalto. Clearly his deepest influence became Le Corbusier, absorbing the lessons in the "fluidity of light" and the syntheses of geometry and sculpture offered by Villa Savoye, Ronchamp Cathedral, and Unité d'Habitation.

Thompson's career blossomed quickly. In 1984 he co-founded Thompson Vaivoda & Associates, (TVA Architects) with fellow architects and friends Ned Vaivoda and David Gellos. Two early office buildings in the Portland suburb of Lake Oswego won AIA Honor Awards, as did an early residential commission. Then investor/arts patrons Donna Drummond and Jeff Alden commissioned a house that further advanced both Thompson's architectural thinking and his career.

The steep hillside site left only a skinny building pad between street and its expansive "backyard," the Hoyt Arboretum. Thompson pulled the house back from the street with a narrow courtyard and lap pool for Alden, a dedicated swimmer, screened by a low stucco wall. He clustered the baths and utility rooms into a solid bar along the public side of the house while opening the living, dining room, and bedrooms out to the distant views of the wooded arboretum beyond. Two cylindrical skylights further welcomed the shifting sunlight through the entire course of the day. The house established an early vocabulary of proportion, volumes, and forms—with light and shadow as a primary architectural actor—that anticipates much of Thompson's other work, residential and larger, that followed.

"When I look back across my career, it's incredible how important the early houses were in developing my preoccupation with human scale, geometry, volume, and a fixation on detailing—making sure everything aligned and flowed," Thompson says.

Thompson's growing reputation in the northwest and awards captured the attention of Nike's co-founder Phil Knight who invited him to compete in a national competition with four other firms to design his growing company's first headquarters. Then a $700-million company with a thousand employees, Nike was strewn across 27 small buildings throughout the Portland metro area. Knight selected Thompson who was only 32 at the time, which marked the beginning of a continuing 30-year relationship.

"The first phase of the campus was all about placemaking," Thompson recalls, "about what we could do with very simple cost-driven buildings to create a new corporate home that spoke to the company brand and culture." Besides adaptability, Knight believed the architecture should be neutral, simple, and understated, laboratories that facilitated the incubation of new ideas and innovation in product development. While satisfying his client, the architect willed into being a campus that soon became nearly as iconic as the brand: the first series of buildings coincided with the explosive revenues and influence of the Michael Jordan brand and Wieden+Kennedy's "JUST DO IT" campaign. With the campus as a capstone to his first six years of work, Thompson became the nation's youngest architect to be inducted into the American Institute of Architect's College of Fellows, the institute's highest honor.

Thompson doesn't render; he draws plans and elevations. More interested in volume than structure, he uses bold sketches and color to divine volumes into mass. His study models bring the drawings to dimension and gradually into a study of light and shadow. In his early work, Thompson's facility in two dimensions served him well. Steerage-ticket budgets, particularly on large projects, often squeeze an architect's actual design work into the thin zone between the maximum leasable space and the envelope allowed by code—the 12-or-so inches between the Sheetrock and exterior cladding. Thompson skillfully and consistently divined the dynamism of his elevations into façades that, like 215 NW Park, in space were nothing more than highly articulated metal extrusions against the flat fields of glass.

In Nike's earliest buildings, the bilateral symmetry and contrast of windows and white cladding stood proud with the optimism of sport. In Thompson's first high-rise, the Fox Tower, an entirely speculative office building for the developer Tom Moyer's first urban project, his graphic clarity served the tight budget well, the similarly stark graphic contrasts accentuating relatively minor variations in mass.

"I've always had this thing about clarity," Thompson says. "When I study people's work, I'm always looking at the programmatic clarity of how the plan drives the envelope. But I also really appreciate the sculptural aspect, how the plan becomes geometric, and the pieces fit together."

As Thompson's client list grew, and loyalists like Phil Knight and Tom Moyer gained greater confidence, so did his budgets. But equally importantly, building technologies and performance metrics gave Thompson greater dimensional latitude. On a simple level, louvers, vertical metal ribs, screens, and integrated curtain walls expand the envelope's usual palette of architectural possibility. The Ford Alumni Center at UO, for instance, offers a softly layered composition of these elements that seems to shimmer against its surroundings. The Murphy Corporate Headquarters in Eugene is similarly shaped to shield the sun but in materials unusually varied for Thompson's work: LVL timber and wood veneers that are manufactured by the company. In the last decade, Thompson has deployed a wide range of these maneuvers to create a series of apartment buildings that stand out nearly as distinctly from their peers in multifamily housing as his private residential commissions do from standard modern houses.

The workplace's evolution from isolated offices and fields of cubicles to mobility, community, and collaboration has also empowered Thompson to develop his passion for soaring interior volumes and powerful axial relationships into gathering places for workers to promenade, convene, and simply enjoy the panoramas of humans in architecture, what Thompson describes as "the circulation being a gallery for human interaction." He's regularly deployed this concept at scales large and small, both in the interiors of buildings, and the outdoor spaces between.

Barely having completed the first phase of Nike's headquarters, Thompson soon began work on a seven-building Phase 2 expansion with Knight now comfortably viewing the company as a legacy brand. Knight wanted the headquarters to be much like a college campus. He wanted a workplace environment where you could come and immerse yourself in all different aspects of life beyond simply work—social interaction, working out, collaborating, developing relationships. The grandest of these later "North Campus" buildings, completed in 2001, have an industrial openness, scale, and muscularity reminiscent of the Deutscher Werkbund, anchored by the Bo Jackson Fitness Center and the Mia Hamm Design Center,

the latter built, in Bauhausian spirit, house all of Nike's design teams. Overall, Thompson more tightly organized this campus, clustering the seven central buildings in a village-like design inspired by Zurich's town center and the public squares of Rome.

With Sony Ericsson Headquarters, Thompson and Gellos lined much of the circulation inside and out with sumptuous expanses of Texas limestone for a powerful backdrop to the employees' arrival and movement inside reminiscent of Richard Meier's Getty Institute. In a soaring central space for the Banfield Pet Hospital corporate headquarters, Thompson centered the vertical circulation in a series of zigzagging ramps—yes, for wheelchairs, but the real driver for their architectural prominence was for the circulation as display of the staff members walking their own 100-plus dogs routinely on-site.

Arguably, two of the greatest tests of Thompson's architectural agility also became his two most prominent buildings. The Matthew Knight Arena not only replaced the alumni's beloved, historic "Mac Court," but also effectively created a new campus gateway, a controversial demand of the arena's funder, Phil Knight, a multi-billion-dollar benefactor of the university. Mid-design, Knight's son, Matthew died, deepening the personal investment. For Thompson the commission became an opportunity to demonstrate the intimacy and human scale of how the old arena could be grown into a larger "theater for basketball" capable of hosting the NCAA Finals. "Knight wanted a building that spoke to the future, spoke to technology, spoke to a more youthful innovative design," Thompson recalls. "He wanted to look forward versus backwards, and obviously he had a lot of pull." Thus, the arena, coupled with Thompson's adjacent Ford Alumni Center, powerfully broke from the "Pattern Language" ethos that had pinched the campus's development since the 1970s. The result offers a stunning example of "circulation as display" with the seating bowl wrapped in vertical expanses of glass that becomes a curvilinear paean to Thompson's earliest architectural experience, the Memorial Coliseum.

The Park Avenue West high-rise required a different kind of dexterity. Started in 2007 as another Moyer office building, the tower construction stalled in the Great Recession. With the exterior envelope already fabricated including the tower glazing warehoused in Shanghai China and aluminum extrusions stored in Korea, Thompson redesigned 50 percent of the interior space into luxury apartments with floor-to-ceiling glass and 10-foot ceilings. Finally completed in 2016, the new tower breathed new life and energy into Portland's central core. At 502 feet, it is Portland's fourth-tallest high-rise, but of any of the city center's tallest towers it has the smallest footprint: 100-by-200 feet. Thompson maximized both the verticality and the responsiveness to its surroundings, sculpting each façade with folds and facets that echo the proportions of the adjacent buildings in four completely distinct faces.

At the foot of Park Avenue West is one of the city's iconic full-block urban public spaces, Director Park. On the eastern edge of the park Fox Tower rises. For Thompson, the ensemble of his towers and plaza pavillions become an "urban campus," proof that context can be respected while being remade.

"I like architecture that stands on its own, that makes a statement," Thompson says, "but not for the sake of, 'Look at me' as much as standing true to itself, elegant, beautifully crafted, simple and understated.

Randy Gragg is a Portland, Oregon—based writer and editor, who has worked in the Pacific Northwest for the past 25 years. He writes about architecture, art, cultural politics, urban design, landscape, and planning.

Top left: Fox Tower, 2000 **Top right:** Mia Hamm Design Center, Nike World Headquarters, 2000 **Bottom:** Nike Asian Corporate Headquarters, 2014

AN ARCHITECTURE OF BALANCE

MICHAEL J. CROSBIE

There is no question that TVA Architects, under the direction of design principal Robert Thompson for nearly 40 years, has made an indelible mark on the architectural character of the Pacific Northwest. Based in Portland, Oregon, the firm has produced work with a presence in most of the region's cities, responding to the context—mindful of local history and building traditions, yet teasing out the unfolding regional identity. Many people gravitate toward the upper-left-hand corner of the continental United States in search of a balance between urban and rural life, a certain cosmopolitanism that also offers some of the most enthralling natural settings North America has to offer. Such connections can be found in TVA's architecture: a celebration of natural materials in the way they are detailed and finished, building envelopes that open themselves to natural light and the crisp air, abundant expanses of glazing that present views of distant mountains, waterways, and timberlands as backgrounds to a thriving civic life that attracts those who desire an urban vibe with close proximity to oceanside and woods, flora, and fauna.

It cannot be denied that Thompson's oeuvre presents an homage to modern masters and their works closely identified with this place (particularly Portland), architects such as John Yeon, Pietro Belluschi, Robert Frasca. Belluschi's Equitable Building (now known as the Commonwealth Building), completed in 1948, is a landmark in the development of post-war high-rise curtainwall design. It's a building that Thompson passes nearly every day and its influence is certainly detectable in TVA's portfolio: architectural solutions distinguished by their clarity, simplicity, and craft. At the same time, Thompson's on-going work for more than three decades with the sports attire retailer Nike, with projects in North America and in Asia, reveals how architecture and branding can meld seamlessly.

A key to TVA's success as a design firm lies in human relationships, both with its clients and the people who populate the practice. Thompson notes that about 85 percent of the firm's work is for repeat clients—an astonishing figure that speaks volumes about the care these architects lavish on their work, the people they design for, and their striving to exceed expectations. Each project is pursued as a collaboration between client and architect, and TVA has cultivated relationships focused on expressing how clients see themselves, their values, and how the architecture reflects them. The built work is a testament to the extent to which client wishes are consistently surpassed—in a sense, the built work "recommends" the architects to repeat and future clients. "There is no better marketer of your work than an inspired client," observes Thompson.

As is true for many exceptional architecture firms, the practice encourages a collegial culture. Many in the firm have made long-term commitments to TVA, some have worked there a quarter-century or more. Thompson describes the coterie of colleagues this way: "Since the inception of our firm in 1984 we have been a collaborative team of friends and colleagues who share a deep passion for design with a commitment to creating meaningful works of architecture that are both moving and inspiring."

Creating outstanding architecture is challenging, but building a successful design practice is even more so. It requires attention, empathy with one's clients and collaborators, and valuing the human interactions at the core of worthy built environments. The architecture documented and presented in this wonderful book shows how it's done.

Michael J. Crosbie *is Professor of Architecture at the University of Hartford and the author of numerous books and articles on architecture.*

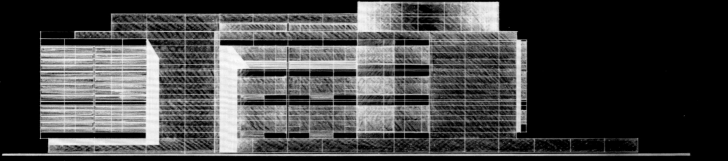
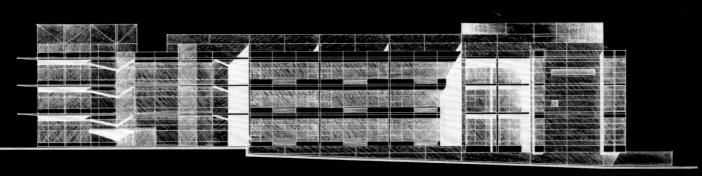
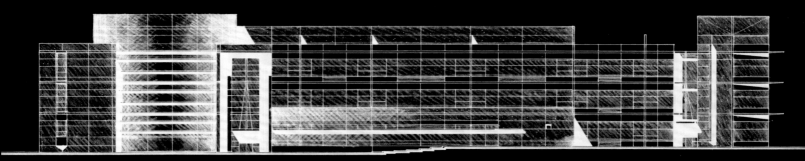

FORD ALUMNI CENTER

EUGENE, OREGON | 2011 | 62,700 SQ FT | LEED GOLD

The University of Oregon Ford Alumni Center functions as the welcome center for prospective students, returning alumni, and campus visitors. Working in tandem with the new Matthew Knight Arena, the Alumni Center building offered our firm and the university an opportunity to create a new front door to the campus, and provide the first impression of the school's distinct identity and core values of progressive thinking, education, and environmental stewardship.

Designed to celebrate the legacy of past alumni and to be the first stop for new inquiries about the university, the Ford Alumni Center expresses a dynamic and forward-looking environment while also affording a link to the past through an interactive interpretive center and a history library. The four-story LEED Gold building houses a large linear sky-lit lobby and lounge, conference rooms, and multipurpose gathering spaces, as well as office space for the University Foundation and other staff.

Programmed after excavation began for a sub-surface parking structure beneath the building site, the project required careful planning to be supported by the pre-existing structural system. The below-ground parking structure allowed the surface area surrounding both the Alumni Center and arena to be utilized as gathering and event spaces rather than for surface parking, creating a dynamic and flexible event site.

The building takes many aesthetic clues from the adjacent arena, but does not mimic it. Rather, it is a direct response to the program within and the experiential and climatic conditions of the site. The building volumes are a clear expression of the public, gallery, and office functions within. Clad in composite metal panels and ribbed-metal siding, the façades also embody a direct response to the solar conditions of the site. Strong vertical and horizontal metal grilles and mesh screens are oriented appropriately for maximum sun control at the large expanses of glass, which offer transparency into and out of the structure.

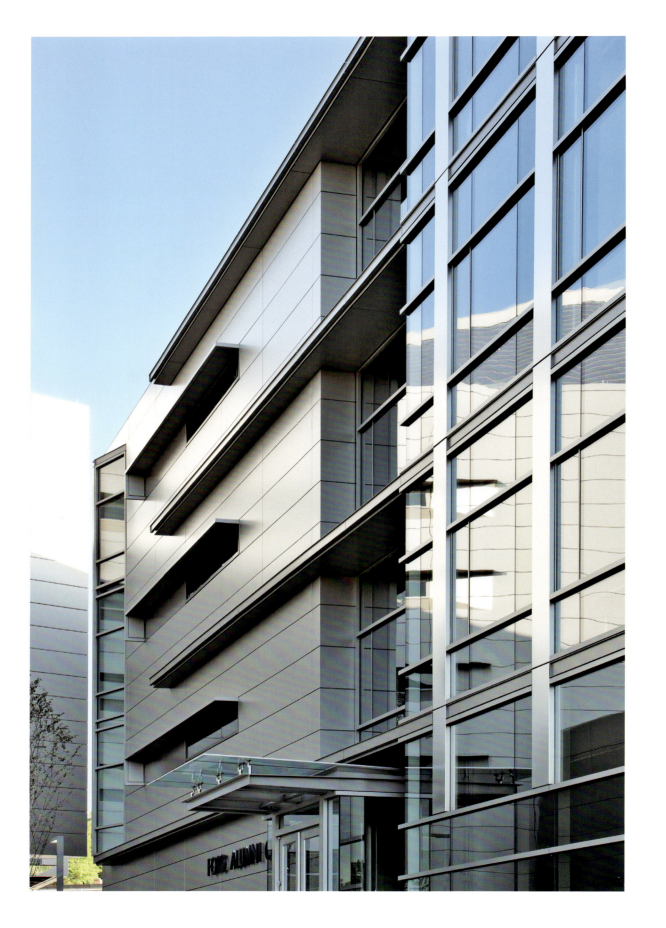

FORD ALUMNI CENTER

FORD ALUMNI CENTER

The skylight running through the building above the lobby atrium provides soft interior natural light throughout the day and is a clear and bold element separating the public and private programmatic spaces on either side. Interior circulation surrounds the atrium, and stairways and landings are easily identifiable and offer places for small gatherings.

The alumni center houses a great hall (the second largest on campus) adjacent to the Donald R. Barker landscaped courtyard that is suitable for formal and informal gatherings for the entire university. The gardens adjacent to the building contain storm-water planters affording users an understanding of the rainwater treatment process. The Ford Alumni Center is also used as a reception area for arena activities and all of the shared outdoor plaza spaces become activated during arena events.

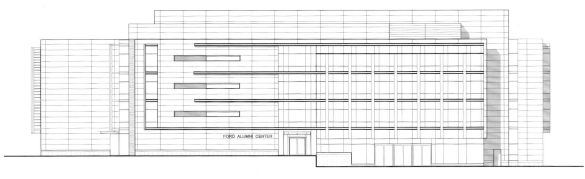

EAST ELEVATION

FORD ALUMNI CENTER

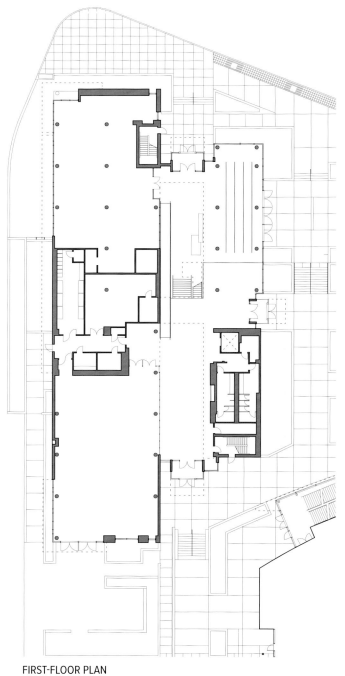

FIRST-FLOOR PLAN

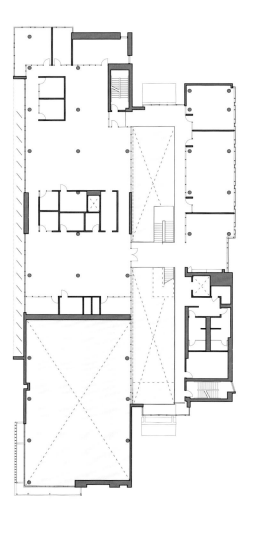

FOURTH-FLOOR PLAN

The skylight running through the building provides natural light throughout the day.

The façades are clad in vertical and horizontal metal grilles that are oriented appropriately for maximum sun control.

BANFIELD CORPORATE HEADQUARTERS

VANCOUVER, WASHINGTON | 2016 | 230,000 SQ FT | LEED PLATINUM

Banfield Pet Hospital is a generational organization with a long-term vision. In developing their corporate headquarters, they sought to build a healthy, collaborative environment that would reflect the Banfield culture, corporate values, and respect for the environment, and also support both employees and their animals.

Banfield's initial intent was to commission a building that would house all departments on a single floor plate; however, through the process of presenting multiple design alternatives I was able to convince the corporate leaders to consider multifloor office buildings instead. This approach would allow for a denser master plan with more site available for outdoor access. The three-building scheme, with a fourth building dedicated to common functions, facilitated a better workplace environment. Each building floor is identical to allow for ease of expansion and contraction of departments. With over 800 employees and more than 220 dogs that come to work periodically, the building was designed to facilitate movement and encourage collaboration. A large atrium space provides key internal connections and contains a three-story ramp that is easy on canine paws, facilitating regular interactions of people as well.

Green features have allowed the company to cut energy use by 44 percent. A geothermal energy exchange heats and cools the interiors, and LED lighting throughout helps reduce the power draw. The campus collects more than 420,000 gallons of rainwater per year for toilet flushing and site irrigation. The building's floor-to-ceiling windows pull daylight into every part of the workspace, and solar panels contribute to the sustainability goals.

BANFIELD CORPORATE HEADQUARTERS

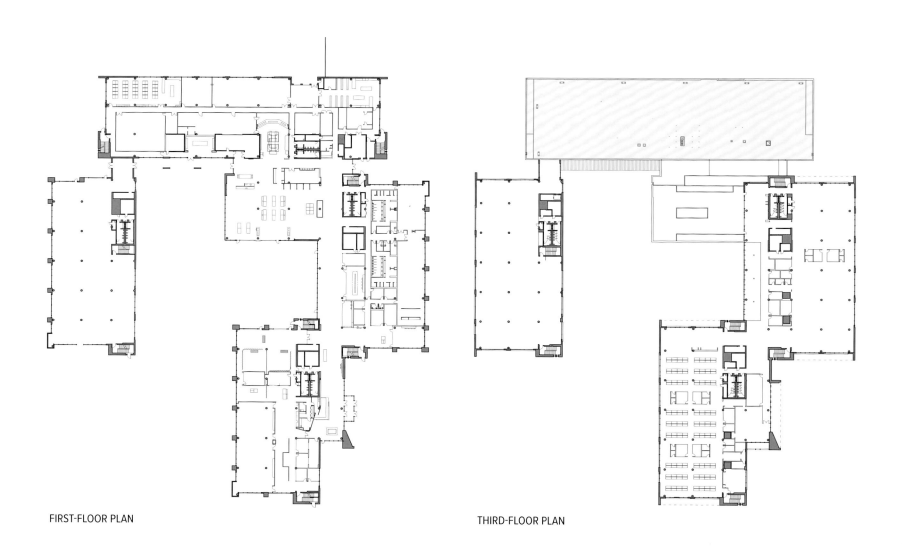

FIRST-FLOOR PLAN

THIRD-FLOOR PLAN

Green features such as insulating green vertical walls and floor-to-ceiling windows have allowed the company to cut energy use by 44 percent.

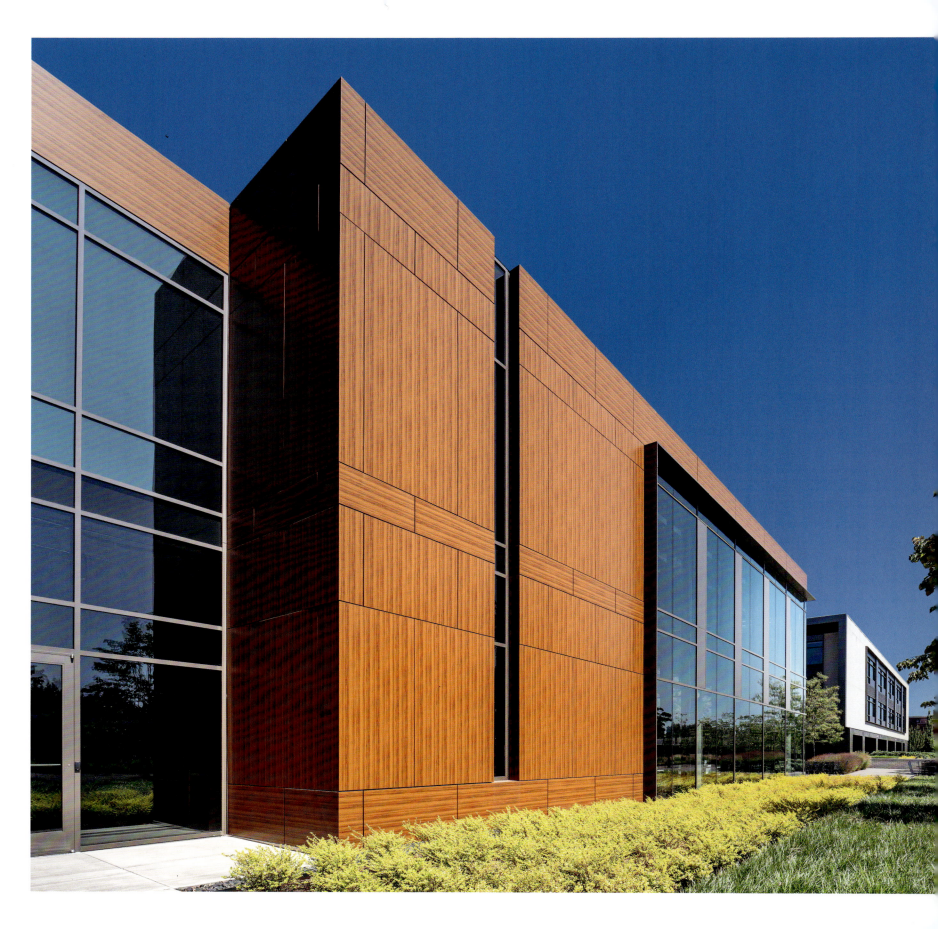

BANFIELD CORPORATE HEADQUARTERS

Outdoor access amid lush landscaping encourages regular staff and canine interaction.

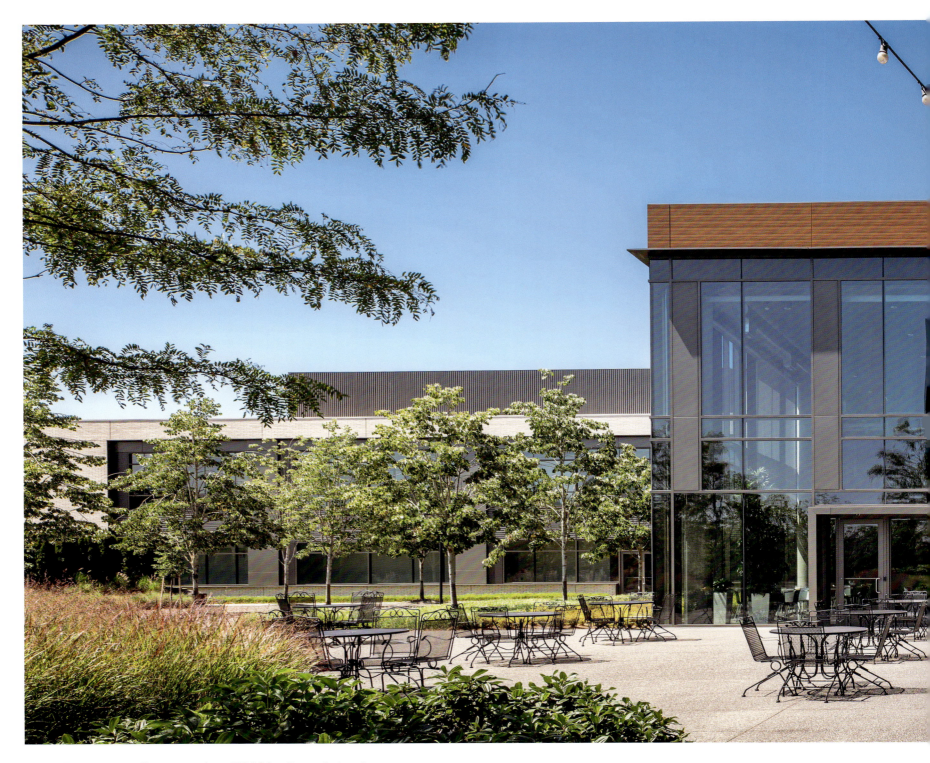

The campus collects more than 420,000 gallons of rainwater per year for toilet flushing and site irrigation.

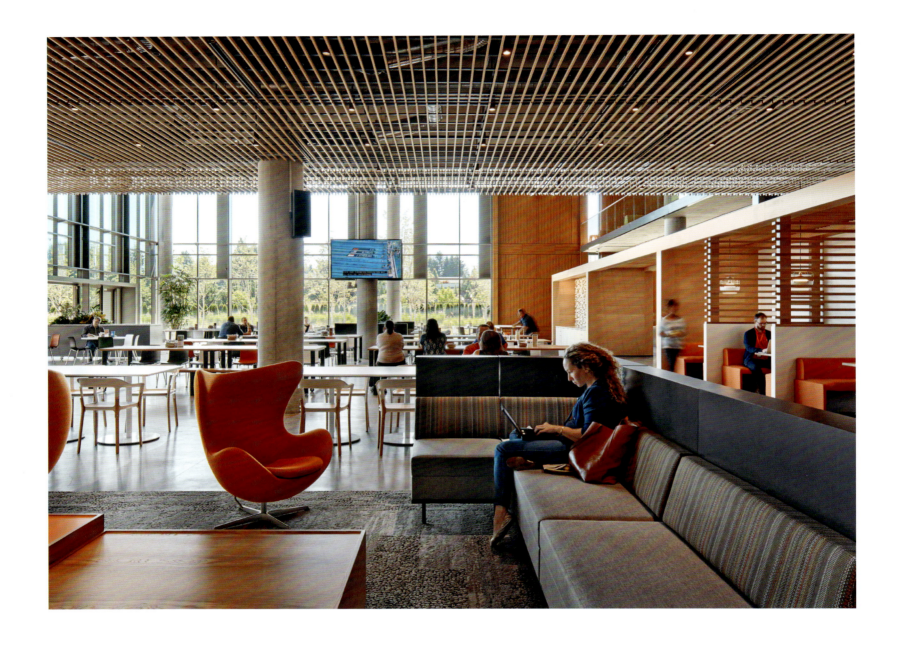

The corporate headquarters encompasses a healthy, collaborative environment while also supporting both employees and their animals.

A large atrium space provides key internal connections and contains a three-story ramp that is easy on canine paws, facilitating regular interactions of people as well.

GSA / SSA CALL CENTER

AUBURN, WASHINGTON | 2007 | 119,000 SQ FT

TVA Architects were selected through a national design competition as the architect for the new General Services Administration (GSA) Headquarters involving the "adaptive reuse" and expansion of a series of abandoned railyard warehouses programmed to house the west coast Social Security Administration (SSA) Call Center located in Auburn, Washington. This became a unique opportunity to honor and respect through preservation the integrity and qualities of these existing structures originally built in the 1940s as industrial warehouses. The opportunity to breathe new life into these structures presented a compelling challenge to recycle and repurpose through sustainable measures these beautiful buildings. With a program originally seeking 80,000 square feet of usable area, we incorporated a 39,000-square-foot mezzanine in the high bay area of the existing building expanding the project to a total of 119,000 square feet of interior area to house the 650 employees who were to occupy the building. I eagerly welcomed the design challenge and respected the goals of the federal government to move beyond the obvious directive of demolishing these structures and to think about how the master-plan design of these multiple warehouse buildings could create a unique workplace environment or campus that could thrive and grow over time into a destination creative office community. The building was renovated under the GSA's "Design Excellence Program" and received a National Honor Award for Design Excellence in the summer of 2006, with the jury describing the completed project as "a gleaming model of sustainability and workplace quality."

GSA / SSA CALL CENTER

The project program called for the adaptive reuse of an abandoned railyard warehouse to be converted into a state-of-the-art headquarters for the GSA / SSA west coast call center housing 650 employees.

GSA / SSA CALL CENTER

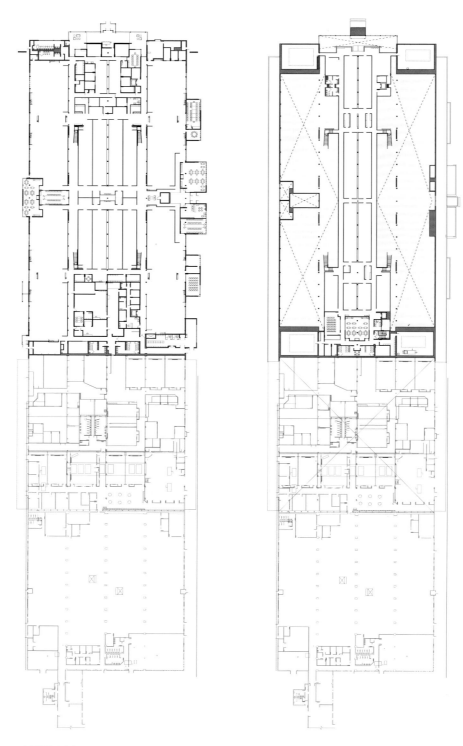

FIRST-FLOOR PLAN

SECOND-FLOOR PLAN

The addition of a mezzanine in the high bay area expanded the project interior area to house the 650 employees.

The renovated building received a National Honor Award for Design Excellence, with the jury describing the completed project as "a gleaming model of sustainability and workplace quality."

METRO HEADQUARTERS

PORTLAND, OREGON | 1994 | 198,000 SQ FT

In 1992, Metro, Portland's regional governmental agency, outgrew its existing facility and elected to develop new consolidated offices by renovating an existing vacated Sears department store. Originally built in 1929, the building had been further modified by five additions and a renovation before being completely clad in a precast "marble crete" skin. The client's programmatic intent was to develop a strong, graphic building image that spoke to a modernist approach that was visually accessible to the public, that set itself apart from other governmental agencies, and that tied together the five building additions into a single unified complex. Additionally, Metro required the renovation to be a demonstration project for building product reuse and recycling.

The extremely large retail floor plans and tight column spacing resulted in dark interior spaces. The solution was to demolish the center bay, creating a light-filled atrium and a simple interior circulation spine flanked by common programmatic elements such as restrooms, conference rooms, and private offices. The effective perimeter bay depth for open-office systems was thus decreased, affording all employees views and abundant natural light.

Working within the existing 24-square-foot column grid, the exterior skin was stripped to the existing concrete frame and manipulated to create a strong exterior skin of glass and aluminum window bays. The scheme provided multiple retail opportunities at the sidewalk level. Due to the mass of the existing building, special attention was given to the exterior elevations, reducing them to a defined building base, midsection, and top. Trellised roof terraces and the redevelopment of the existing water tower for employee lounges and a conference room cap the building. The light-color brick was chosen to complement neighboring buildings, while the articulation of the aluminum and glass grid plays to the tension of the towers of the nearby Convention Center.

At the northern end of the site a former parking lot now functions as an entry plaza for public events and employee gatherings. Entry to the plaza occurs at the street corner where it is defined by a steel trellis that slices through a small retail pavilion on the corner. Large stamped aluminum screens from the existing building were used to mask the plaza from the adjacent parking structure while large raised landscape planters break down the scale of the exterior space creating an intimate urban park. Located below street level, two former retail floors have been converted into 285 parking stalls available to Metro employees.

The redevelopment of the existing water tower for employee lounges and a conference room cap the building.

METRO HEADQUARTERS

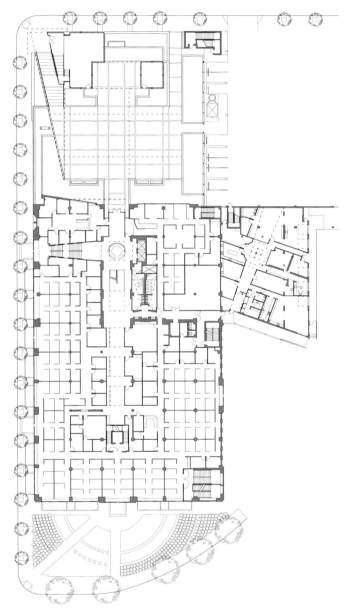

FIRST-FLOOR PLAN

SECOND-FLOOR PLAN

The striking renovation of an old 1929 Sears store resulted in a modern publicly accessible building that tied together the existing five building additions into a single unified complex.

MURPHY CORPORATE OFFICES

EUGENE, OREGON | 2019 | 15,000 SQ FT

Founded in 1909, Murphy is one of the oldest family-owned forest product fabricators in the United States. My long association with the Murphy family and our love of locally sourced building materials were instrumental as we helped them expand their headquarters and develop a new public face. Sited adjacent to their existing production facility, the new administrative building is a light-filled environment that will support the next generation of growth for one of Oregon's leading suppliers of architectural plywood veneers and structural LVL timber. Integrating seamlessly into the design and structure of the project, we incorporated Murphy's products to highlight the incredible beauty and function of wood.

The industrial character of the surrounding warehouse district informed our choice of dark, ribbed-metal panels for the exterior cladding. Organized along an east–west axis to maximize solar orientation, deep window recesses and vertical aluminum fins control sun exposure and provide shading. High glass relites at private offices allow transparency through the building, to the landscaping beyond. A modern, minimalist landscape was developed to provide visual interest throughout the year. Large drifts of low ornamental grasses, swoops of native plants, and an allée of Jacquemontii Himalayan birch trees are key elements of the landscape.

The new administrative headquarters is designed to facilitate the next generation of company growth. The building and its interior work environment are an expression of simplistic understated elegance constructed from finish materials manufactured by the company.

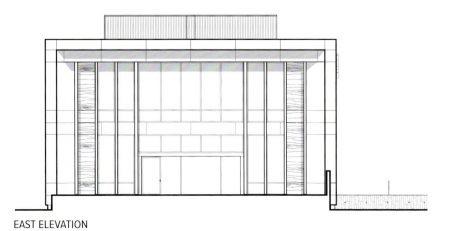

EAST ELEVATION

MURPHY CORPORATE OFFICES

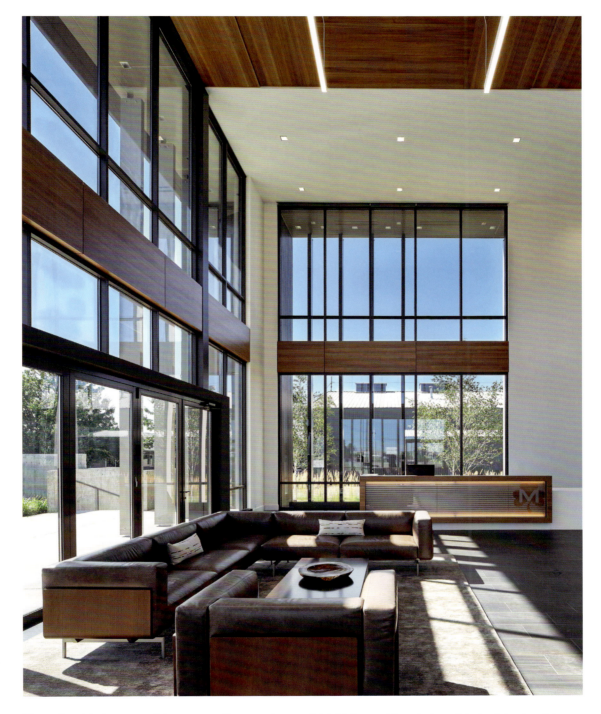

The industrial character of the surrounding warehouse district informed the choice of dark, ribbed-metal panels for the exterior cladding. Large glazed panels with deep window recesses and vertical aluminum fins control sun exposure and provide shading.

MURPHY CORPORATE OFFICES

FIRST-FLOOR PLAN

SECOND-FLOOR PLAN

The interior layout called for perimeter offices with a central open skylight spine accommodating clerical and support functions.

The staircase showcases the products of one of Oregon's leading suppliers of architectural plywood veneers and structural LVL timber. High glass relites at private offices allow transparency through the building, to the landscaping beyond.

NIKE ASIAN CORPORATE HEADQUARTERS

SHANGHAI, CHINA | 2014 | 650,000 SQ FT | LEED GOLD

Situated on a repurposed airfield that makes it one of the first brownfield developments in Shanghai, the campus is adjacent to a 33-acre ecological park reserve.

Looking to unite its Asia operations after doing business in China for over 30 years, Nike wished to create a new headquarters that took East/West collaboration to the next level. The Nike Asian Corporate Headquarters is a new multibuilding campus for Nike's research and development efforts in Asia, designed to support Nike's long-term business growth strategy in China. To highlight to the region what is possible through sustainable practices, Nike chose to create a "green" community.

The campus consists of a Phase 1 nine-story, 420,000-square-foot office building, a 240,000-square-foot multipurpose showroom/conference center as well as a Nike Retail store and campus reception center. Along with the commercial buildings, it features a soccer pitch, regulation-size indoor basketball court, and state-of-the-art fitness facility. The campus houses a full-service food and beverage facility and the standalone conference center hosts large-scale events and product unveilings.

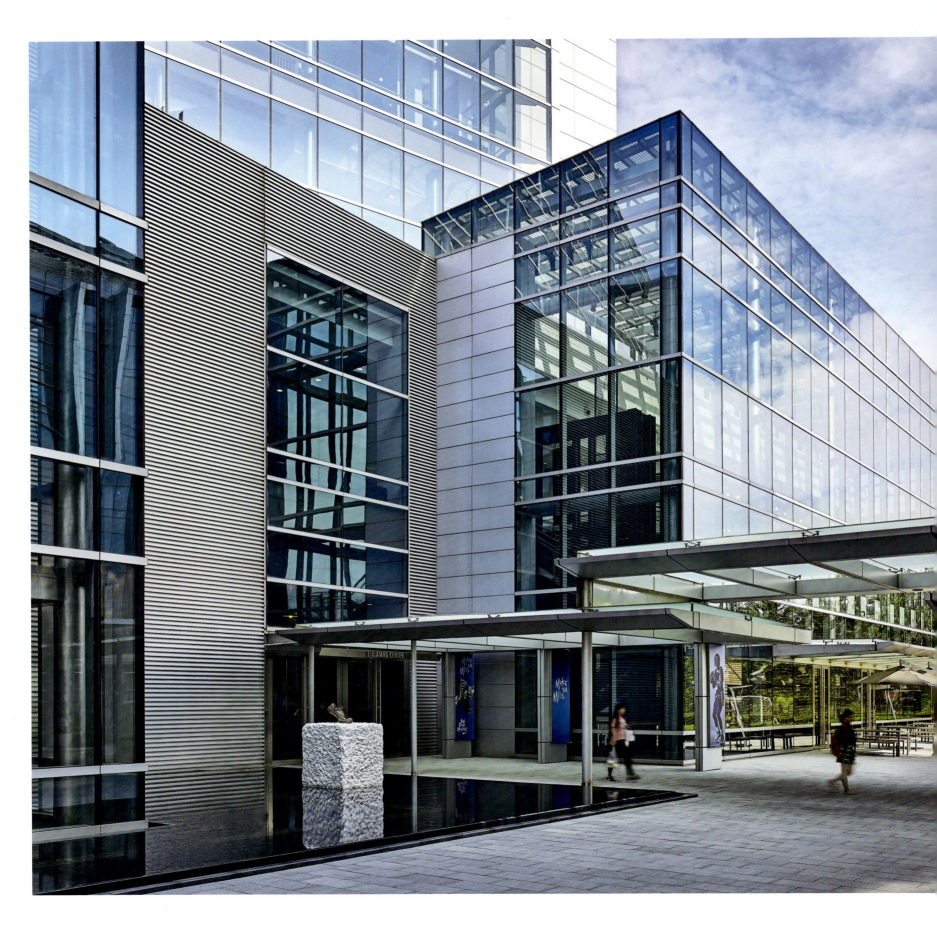

NIKE ASIAN CORPORATE HEADQUARTERS

The Shanghai campus has been designed as a "green" community focused on sustainable practices that make it an environmental leader in the city.

Phase 1 of the campus consists of three major buildings, including offices, a major product showroom and conference center, as well as a reception building that embraces a central soccer pitch as the organizing plan feature.

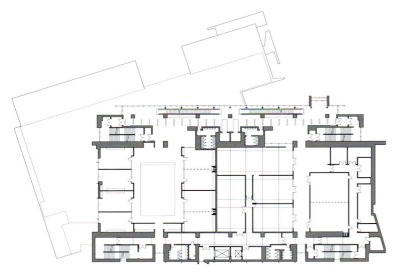

CONFERENCE CENTER FOURTH-FLOOR PLAN

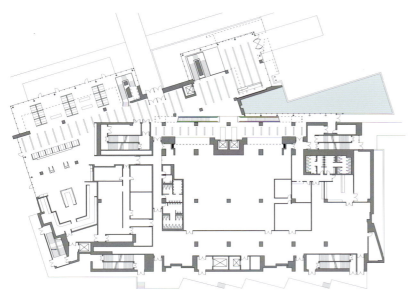

CONFERENCE CENTER FIRST-FLOOR PLAN

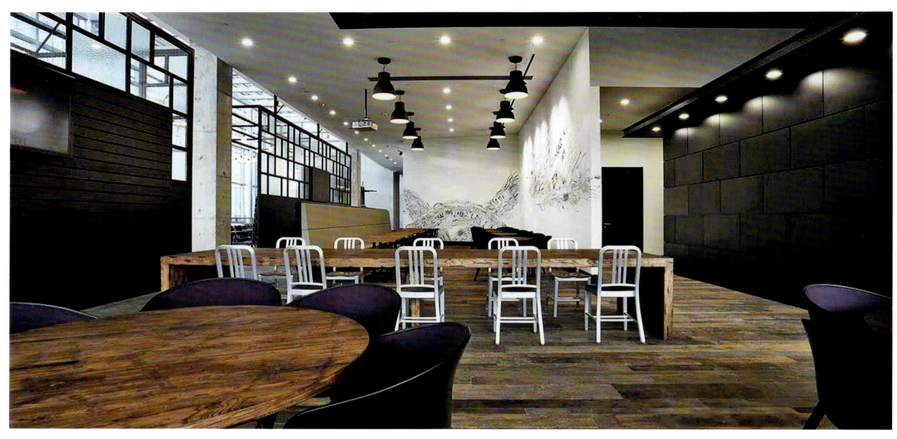

The state-of-the-art interiors are designed to maximize staff collaboration and to support Nike's long-term business growth in Asia.

NIKE ASIAN CORPORATE HEADQUARTERS

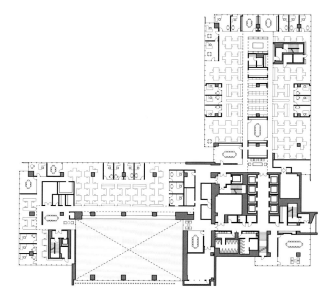

OFFICE BUILDING SECOND-FLOOR PLAN

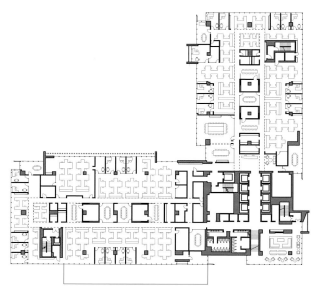

OFFICE BUILDING THIRD-FLOOR PLAN

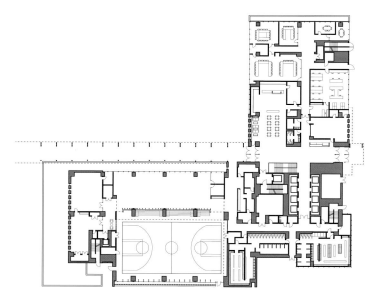

OFFICE BUILDING FIRST-FLOOR PLAN

The Shanghai headquarters is a new multibuilding campus for Nike's research and product development efforts in Asia, including a nine-story office building housing 750 employees.

SONY ERICSSON HEADQUARTERS

PLANO, TEXAS | 2001 | 520,000 SQ FT

In 1998, Sweden-based Sony Ericsson, Inc. chose to consolidate its multiple leases in the Dallas area and create a new headquarters for its American division in the Legacy Corporate Park in Plano, Texas. Following a nationwide tour of corporate campuses, Sony Ericsson staged a planning competition for a 1.5-million-square-foot corporate campus to be constructed in three equal phases. The 110-acre master plan that evolved is a sympathetic response to the regional climate, natural landscape elements, and site conditions of the location and provide its unique character. These elements have guided the solution and have described a planning direction that reinforces the marriage of built and natural landscape environments.

The Phase I development establishes a framework that permits multiple development and construction options for future corporate growth. Phase I encompasses 36.65 acres, or roughly a third of the entire site. However, it utilizes the middle sector, capturing a majority of the upper lake and, with an easement to the east, has access from all four frontages. This quickly establishes a hierarchy of entrance: visitors will use the formal entry from Legacy Drive, while employees will enter from Corporate Drive and Tennyson, and service vehicles from Communications Parkway.

The parking plan arranges parking rows concentrically about a center in the lake, and mitigates the long parking rows commonly encountered when parking 1,700 cars on ground level. Alternate parking medians contain pedestrian walkways and landscaping of sufficient stature to provide sun protection as pedestrians make their way to the building entries. The center of the diagram is situated such that a transcribed radius penetrates the lobbies of both buildings and extends landscaped walkways to the edges of parking opportunities. These "spokes" serve as pedestrian collectors and funnel people to the employee entries. The parking diagram overlays all phases and serves as another matrix that further cements the phases of the master plan over time.

SONY ERICSSON HEADQUARTERS

The campus land plan focused on the integration and marriage of the buildings into the natural landscape. Surrounding an existing natural lake, on-site offices and common amenity spaces open out onto outdoor plazas and collaborative meeting areas integrated into the landscape.

The main entry drive terminates in an auto court that takes advantage of an existing topographical land shear. This serves the parti well as primary employee entries occur at the second level of the building's exterior perimeter. Mid-level entries will encourage people to use stairs rather than elevators, thus fostering interaction and increasing the activity level. Primary circulation occurs at the first level, along the interior perimeter and adjacent to the lake. This further strengthens the notion of layering and more clearly establishes the division between public and private domains. Internal walking streets, or esplanades, parallel the building elevations that front the lake and energize the heart of the campus/village. All buildings are connected internally, in deference to the Texas summer sun and heat. The Phase 1 plan rests confidently balanced on its own, controlling the best offerings of the site yet anxious to engage the future.

SONY ERICSSON HEADQUARTERS

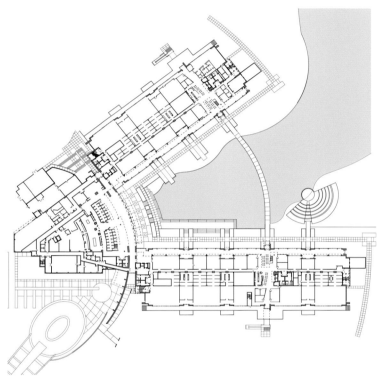

FIRST-FLOOR PLAN

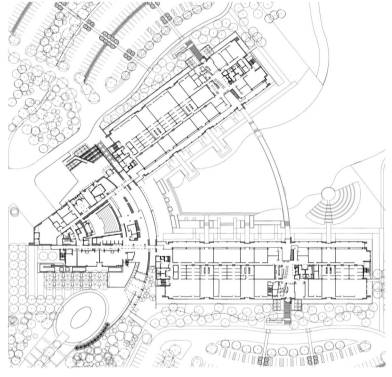

SECOND-FLOOR PLAN

Internal building circulation occurs along the lake edge connecting office space to the common amenity building at the heart of the plan.

PARK AVENUE WEST TOWER

PORTLAND, OREGON | 2016 | 618,000 SQ FT | LEED PLATINUM

Park Avenue West is Portland's newest high-rise office tower built in the city since TVA Architects designed Fox Tower was completed in the year 2000. At 30 stories, the 618,000-square-foot mixed-use tower occupies a prominent site in the heart of Portland's urban core and is composed of a two-story retail base, 17 stories of high-end apartments, and 12 stories of Class A office space. Park Avenue West, along with the Fox Tower which sits adjacent, was designed for my very first client, legendary Portland developer Tom Moyer, whom I met a year after opening the TVA office in 1984.

The architectural massing of the new building is composed of a slender 30-story tower delineated by a strong retail podium, a simple midsection and a well-defined cap. The design of the building with its refined formal vocabulary reflects the distinct orientation of the site while addressing requirements of sustainability, maximum efficiency, and flexibility. At completion, the building was certified with a LEED Platinum energy rating. The north and south façades of the tower are composed of a continuous high performance folded curtain wall that reinforces the slender verticality of the building. The east and west façades are deliberately different and speak to strong horizontal strapping of aluminum panels at each floor that reference the proportions of the surrounding buildings and its context.

The tower entry faces SW 9th Ave to the west and combines both the office and apartment lobbies that share a common seating area focused on a large fireplace that forms the heart of the space. Level 6 contains the amenity floor for the apartments housing two small apartments for guests of the apartment tenants as well as a beautifully crafted common space to support large gatherings and meetings in addition to an outdoor garden terrace that looks over Directors Park to the south. The building's anchor tenant is Portland's largest law firm who occupies the top floors of the tower with access to two large outdoor roof terraces and unparalleled views over the city, the Willamette River, and the Cascade mountain range to the east.

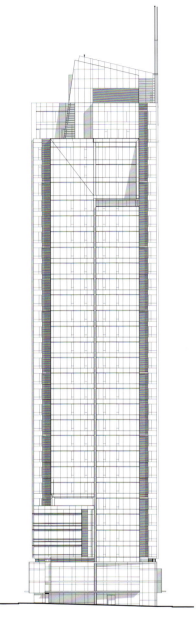

WEST ELEVATION

The 30-story mixed-use tower occupies a prominent site in the heart of Portland's urban core and is composed of a retail base, high-end apartments, and Class A office space.

PARK AVENUE WEST TOWER

The exterior of the tower is clad in composite aluminum panels and a glass curtain wall to give the tower a taut envelope expressing the strong geometric forms of the building. Italian travertine stone clads the exterior entry walls as well as the lobby flooring bringing warmth and softness to the experience of entering the building.

At the same time I was designing Park Avenue West we were commissioned again by Tom Moyer to lead the design of a new six-story 700-car below-ground parking structure on the half block immediately to the south of Park Avenue that also fronted the Fox Tower to the east. The garage would have direct access from the Fox Tower and would serve both towers. As a component to the project, Laurie Olin was commissioned by Portland Parks as landscape architect to design a new pocket park that would occupy the surface of the garage. Robert Frasca with ZGF Architects designed a beautiful glass canopy and I lead the design of two simple, elegant glass pavilions containing elevators and stairs that served the garage below. It was a special opportunity for me to collaborate with Robert on this project, as he was a great mentor of mine in my early days as a young designer in Portland.

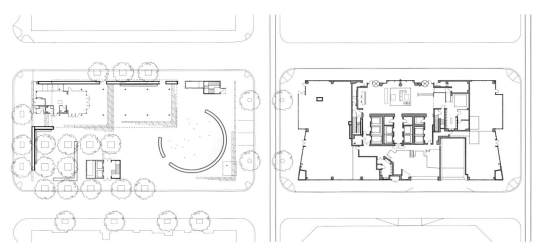

SITE PLAN INCLUDING DIRECTOR PARK PAVILIONS

The tower entry faces SW 9th Ave to the west and combines both the office and apartment lobbies that share a common seating area focused on a large fireplace that forms the heart of the space.

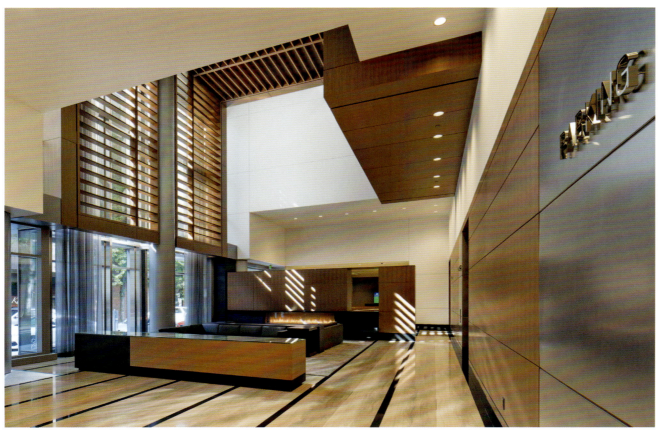

PARK AVENUE WEST TOWER

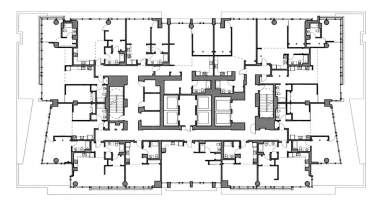

FOURTH-FLOOR PLAN

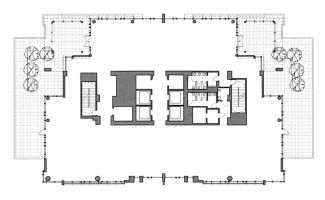

29TH-FLOOR PLAN

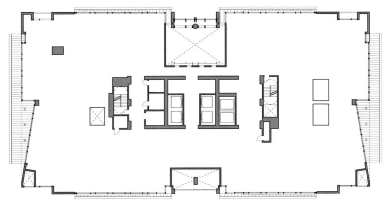

SECOND-FLOOR PLAN

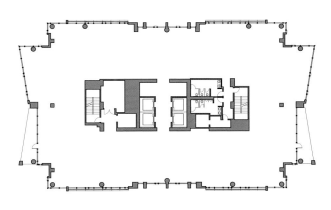

25TH-FLOOR PLAN

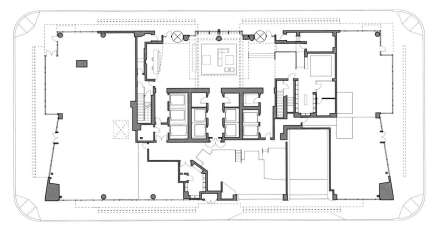

FIRST-FLOOR PLAN

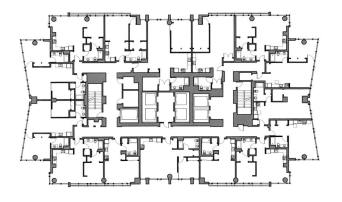

SEVENTH-FLOOR PLAN

FOX TOWER

PORTLAND, OREGON | 2000 | 600,000 SQ FT | LEED GOLD

The Fox Tower was my first introduction to designing a high-rise office tower. It occupies a prominent location in the heart of downtown Portland adjacent to Pioneer Court House Square.

Inspired by the contextual urban fabric of downtown, the 27-story, 600,000-square-foot Fox Tower is rendered and articulated with a sense of proportion and scale that is both comfortably familiar and ultimately timeless. The design of the street level incorporates the wish of both the city and the owner for accessibility and visual exposure. The street level is punctuated with frequent entrances, allowing pedestrians to filter easily into and out of the retail, theater, and office lobby spaces. Extensive glazing at all levels of the tower create open vistas to and from the building, enhancing the exterior façade and creating a friendlier day-lit internal environment.

The Fox Tower massing configuration results from the interplay of simple geometric volumes, creating a composition of three interlocking forms. These forms originate at street level where they engage and interlock with a three-story retail and theater base.

The establishment of the fully glazed central tower element, which is curved on its eastern exposure and stepped on its western exposure, initiates the massing composition of the tower. This taut volume, clad in reflective glazing, is held on the eastern and western façades by orthogonal bookend elements. These massing pieces are given more weight by being clad at the spandrel conditions with a light-colored aluminum panel system, which is, in turn, given additional depth and relief through the introduction of horizontal metal channels and expressed aluminum panel joints.

FOX TOWER

Inspired by their contextual urban surroundings, Thompson's Fox Tower and Park Avenue West Tower convey a sense of proportion and scale that is both comfortably famiiar and ultimately timeless.

FOX TOWER

As the tower form meets grade, it is contained to the east and west by a three-story podium containing retail and theater functions. The massing of these elements reflects a carefully balanced interplay of the open retail components and the necessarily closed nature of the theater spaces. Unique to the Fox Tower design is the significant amount of glazing provided at the retail levels, which is carried to the theater level and encloses the major circulation functions of the theater's program. Visual continuity from the street level through all the base functions is maintained at all street frontages. The base façade is a synthesis of slipping glass and stone planes, punctuated for additional relief by vertical channel and fin elements, adding to the rich quality of the overall façade treatment.

The sum of the parts equals a harmonious and poetic design solution incorporating the complex influences of city, site, pedestrian, transportation, context, and open space. The Fox Tower is designed to comply with the intent of Portland's Central Commercial Zone for construction of large-scale developments that will add energy and vitality to downtown Portland and create a safe and attractive pedestrian-oriented streetscape.

FOX TOWER

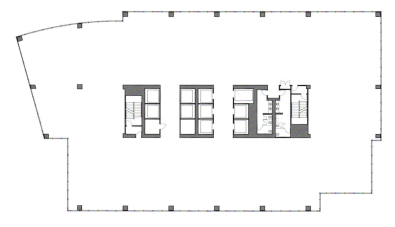

THIRD-FLOOR PLAN

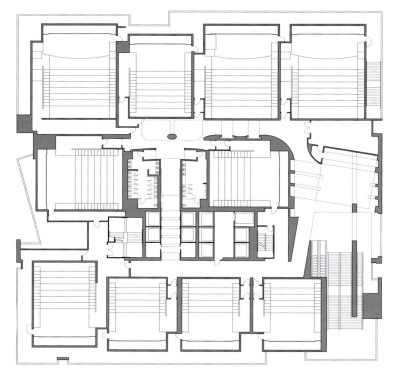

SECOND-FLOOR PLAN

The main building entry bisects the street-level floor plan through a grand two-story lobby that allows circulation mid-block through the building.

VANCOUVER OFFICE TOWER

VANCOUVER, WASHINGTON | COMPLETION TBD | 220,000 SQ FT

The Vancouver Office Tower will occupy a prominate location on the banks of the Columbia River in downtown Vancouver, Washington. This new signature tower located next to the Interstate I-5 bridge will act as a sentinel, a gateway element welcoming people as they enter the State of Washington crossing over the river from Oregon. The 11-story 220,000-square-foot commercial office building will be a new addition to the Vancouver River Front district that is leading the revitalization and redevelopment of downtown Vancouver as it experiences explosive growth in urban housing to accommodate an influx of new people moving to the city.

The structure consists primarily of open-office space, private courtyards and is configured to take maximum advantage of views to the Columbia River. Minimalistic in form, great consideration was given to the materiality, the transparency, and the composition of the tower due to its location adjacent to the river. The tower skin is a taut semitransparent curtain wall used to emphasize the simplistic form and geometry of the building. Windows are maximized in size to full floor-to-floor heights eliminating horizontal breakup of the views out. Shallow vertical aluminum fins articulate the exterior walls adding rich detail, depth and shadow to the building elevations. The building massing is broken into three distinct forms expressing a strong podium or base containing first-floor retail, a midsection housing the office functions and a cap defined by a large open canopy providing shelter over an expansive rooftop amenity terrace. At street level, the podium is designed to promote urban activity by providing space for retail and restaurants that share a large outdoor dining terrace with views over the river. The office tower lobby occupies the northwestern corner of the building with its expansive two-story glazed lobby maximizing transparency and clarity to the front door.

VANCOUVER OFFICE TOWER

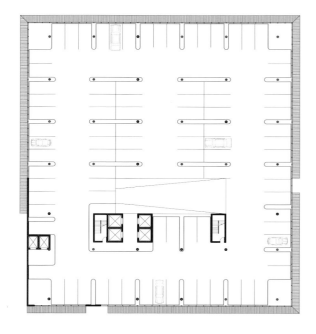

SECOND-FLOOR PLAN

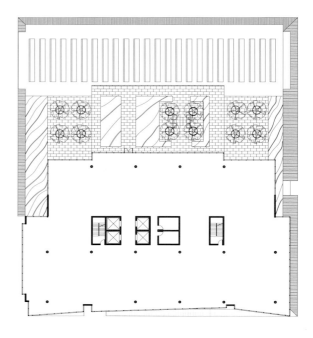

FOURTH-FLOOR PLAN

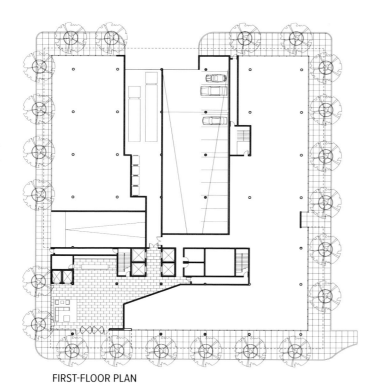

FIRST-FLOOR PLAN

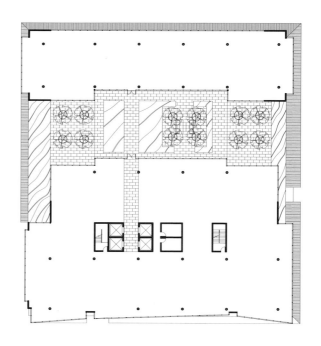

THIRD-FLOOR PLAN

The new signature tower will occupy a prominent location on the banks of the Columbia River and will act as a welcoming gateway element.

OCHOCO AIR HANGAR

HILLSBORO, OREGON | 2015 | 29,750 SQ FT

The Ochoco hangar offered a second opportunity for me to design a private air hangar for a long-term highly valued client. The design brief was for a contemporary aircraft hangar to provide both administrative functions and maintenance facilities to house the owner's private fleet of planes. Challenging us to create an exceptional environment that was visually open but met the strict security requirements dictated by federal and state aviation requirements, as well as his own personal security needs, our client wanted a functional solution that did not compromise luxury. The accelerated schedule necessitated economies of construction that drove the decision to use a manufactured structure. A unique and innovative adaption of a simple Butler Building, the structural frame is covered with composite metal panels and deep, ribbed siding that supports a shaped roof profile.

Sleek and graceful, this aircraft hangar beautifully highlights the jets as one would display objects of art. Tall glass windows provide visibility into the main hangar, as well as visual connectivity to the aircraft from the road beyond. The entire structure sits on an elevated stone podium. A series of tiered walls provide plantings of sustainable native grasses and deciduous trees. The main entrance leads into a passenger waiting area where both owner and guests can comfortably relax before flights. Directly off the main lobby are private offices for pilots and open workstations for mechanics and other flight staff, furnished with custom walnut veneer casework. A large conference room and communal kitchen have oversized steel windows allowing visibility into the main hangar and the jets.

OCHOCO AIR HANGAR

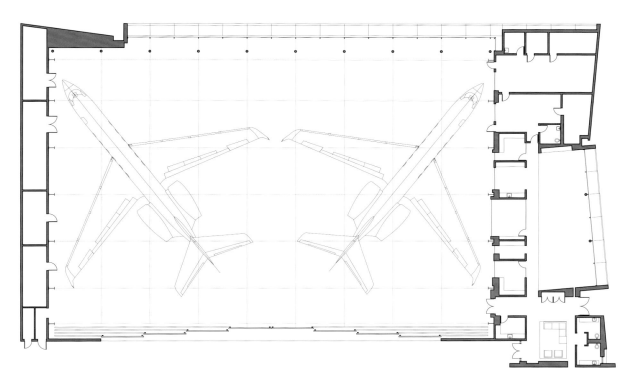

FLOOR PLAN

Tall glass windows from the conference room provide visibility into the main hangar, as well as visual connectivity to the aircraft.

The hangar bay opens out to the adjacent street offering powerful views of the planes.

Directly off the main lobby are private offices for pilots and open workstations for flight staff who share a two-story common workplace. The main entrance leads into a passenger waiting area where both owner and guests can comfortably relax before flights.

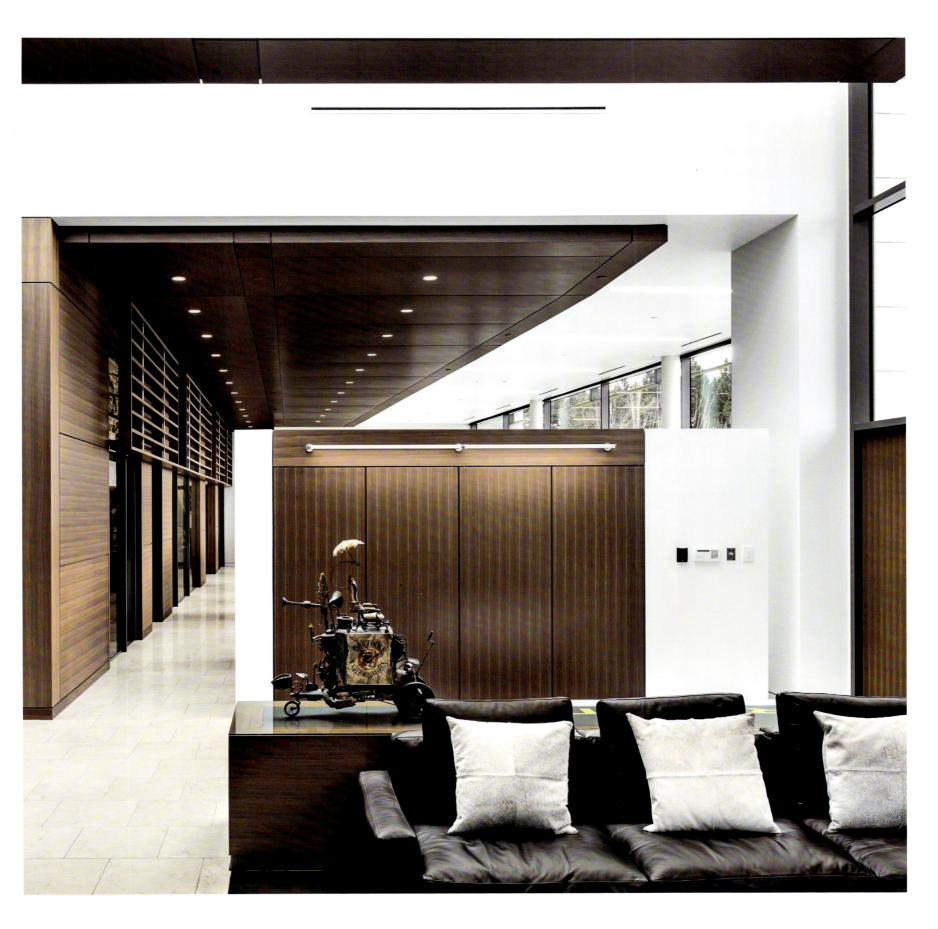

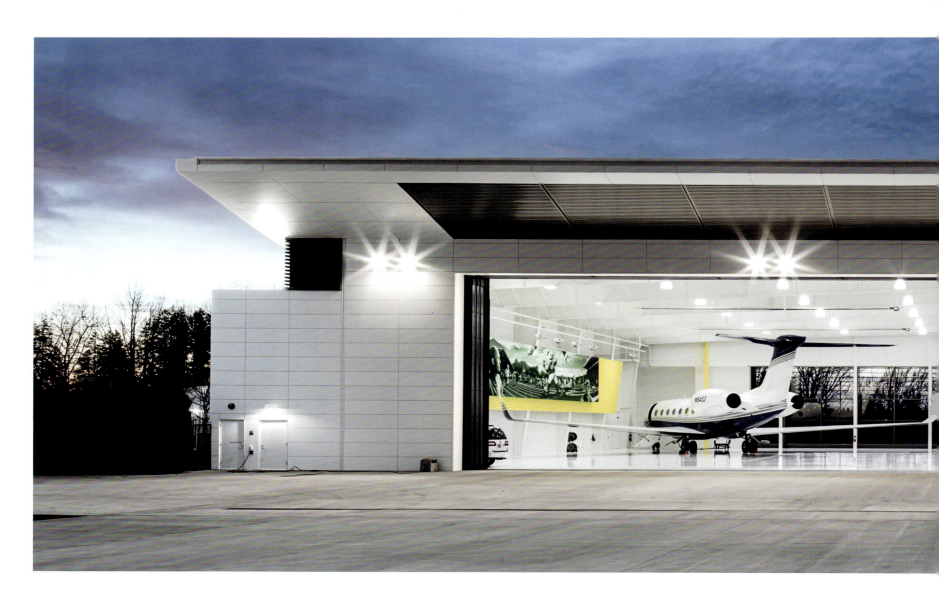

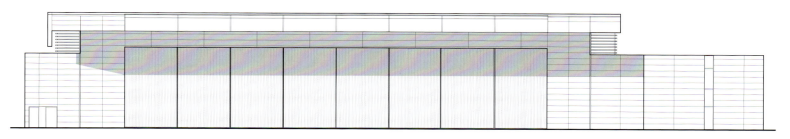

WEST ELEVATION

Sleek and graceful, this aircraft hangar beautifully highlights the jets as one would display objects of art.

OCHOCO AIR HANGAR

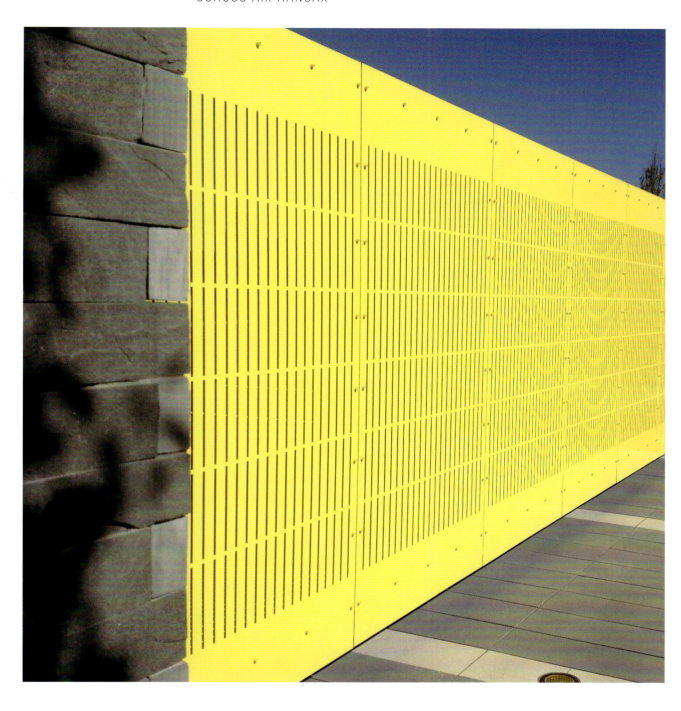

The air hangar is positioned atop a natural stone podium sustainably landscaped with native grasses and trees that reinforce the geometry and architecture of the site. A bright yellow rolling gate separates secured private and public parking.

NIKE AIR HANGAR

BEAVERTON, OREGON | 2002 | 40,000 SQ FT

The Nike Air Hangar is a 40,000-square-foot corporate facility designed to support Nike's global flight operations. Located six miles west of the Nike World Headquarters, the hangar is a simple understated elegant expression of the Nike brand language that has guided that architecture of the company's World Headquarters buildings. The privately owned air facility is designed to house its corporate fleet consisting of three Gulfstream G5 jets for executive business travel. In addition to the requisite support space for flight planning and airplane maintenance, the hangar provides amenities for travelers and pilots, including a spacious waiting lounge, exercise facilities, executive suites, and a gourmet kitchen. It also provides a convenient site for off-campus meetings and private functions. Clad in a tightly ribbed-metal skin the plan and form of the building is intentionally simple consisting of the primary hangar bay in addition to a sidecar building containing pilot offices, conference rooms, fabrications shops, and vehicular storage.

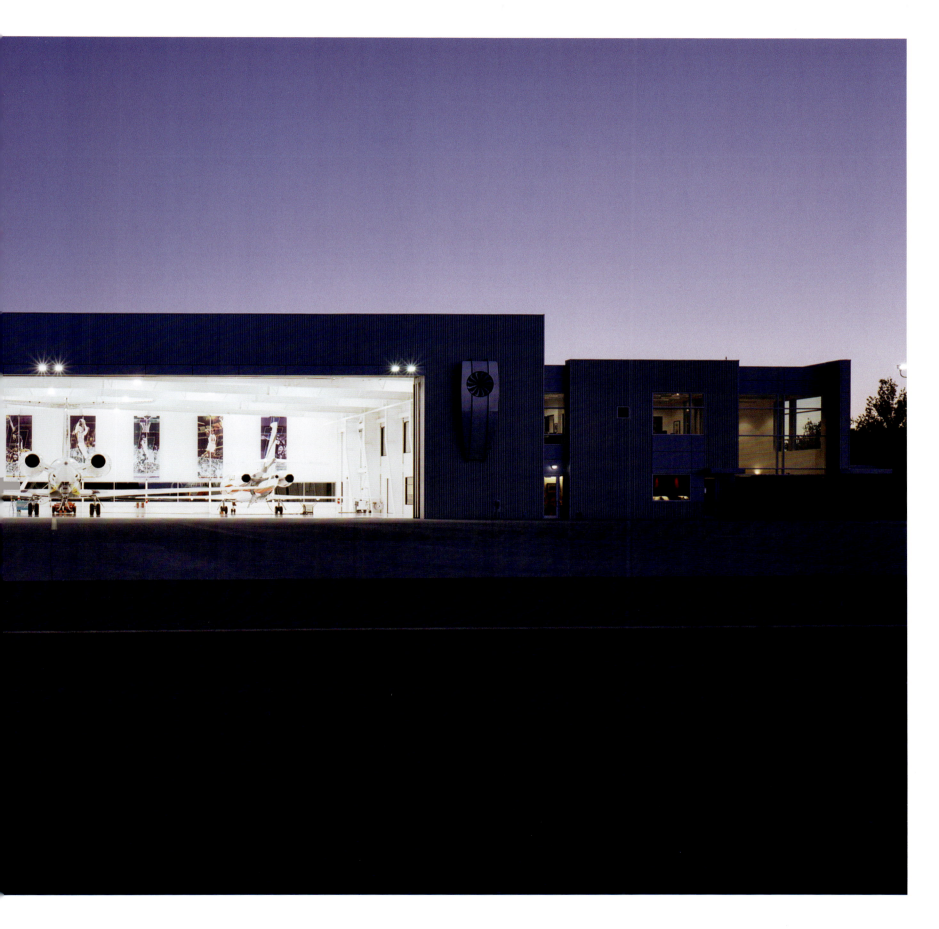

The hangar provides amenities for travelers and pilots, including a spacious waiting lounge, executive suites, and a gourmet kitchen.

NIKE AIR HANGAR

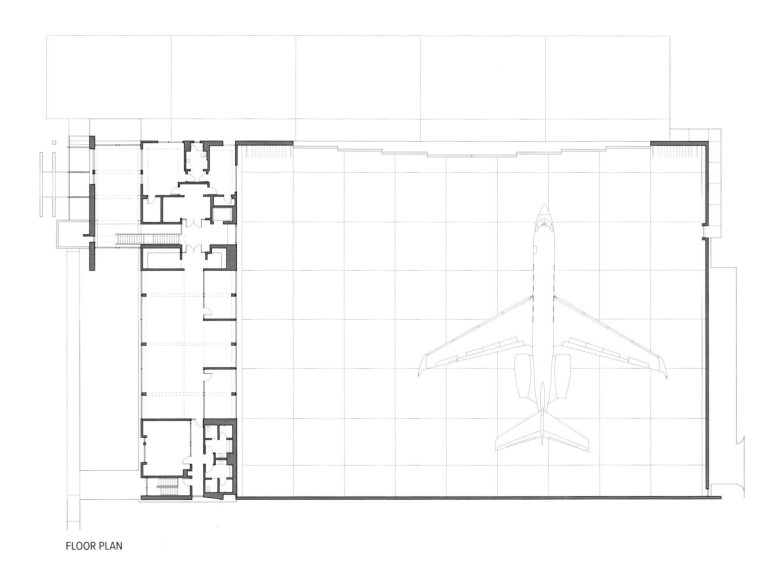

FLOOR PLAN

Clad in a tightly ribbed-metal skin, the plan and form of the building is intentionally a simple understated elegant expression of the Nike brand language.

FORT DALLES TRAINING CENTER

THE DALLES, OREGON | 2014 | 64,500 SQ FT

The Oregon Military Department (OMD) requested a modern facility that addressed contemporary military needs. This project was programmatically complex, as it needed to be secure for OMD but also open and welcoming enough to serve as a community center, a teaching environment, and a venue able to be rented for public functions. Supporting programmatic functions for monthly military training exercises, the spaces include a kitchen, fitness center, administrative offices, weapons vault, simulated firing range, and storage for equipment. The three-story facility also houses a 10,000-square-foot assembly hall, the only one of its size in an Oregon armory.

Because the project is located on the grounds of the Columbia Gorge Community College (CGCC), spaces for the college were incorporated. Intended to provide training in industrial arts for students returning to higher education in search of a second vocation, CGCC created a Workforce Training Center that provides learning environments for electrical, mechanical, welding, and automotive repair. CGCC spaces include four classrooms, two labs, private offices for professors, and a high-bay instructional space featuring a machine shop and welding stations.

With views in practically every direction, the building was designed to amplify the inherent beauty of its location and take advantage of vistas to the Columbia River. Divided in half by a level change of over 30 feet, the existing site was naturally formed into separate plateaus that were used to organize the programmatic elements of the military and the college functions. A butterfly roof soars out over a large glazed façade, and high windows provide natural daylighting to reduce artificial lighting needs. The assembly hall ceiling is a clear-span assembly with deep laminated beams and exposed decking.

FORT DALLES TRAINING CENTER

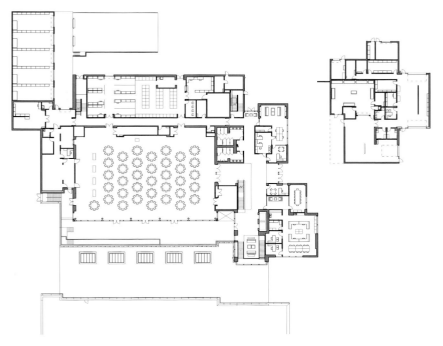

FIRST-FLOOR PLAN

SECOND-FLOOR PLAN

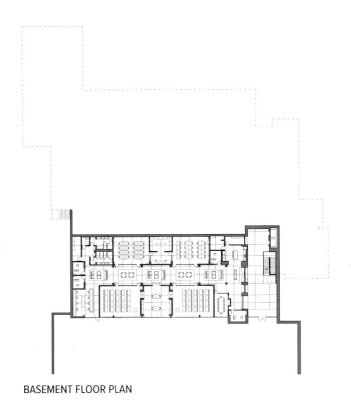

BASEMENT FLOOR PLAN

Thompson's design took great care in maximizing views from all office and community spaces to the Columbia River and Mt. St Helens to the north. Large expanses of glass flood the building with natural light and views throughout the day reinforcing a sense of connection and transparency throughout the building plan.

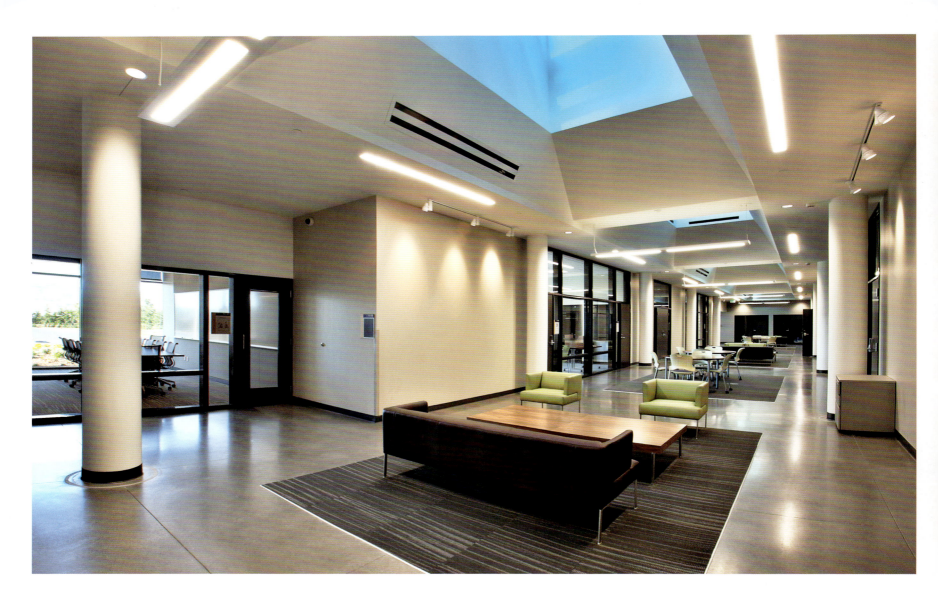

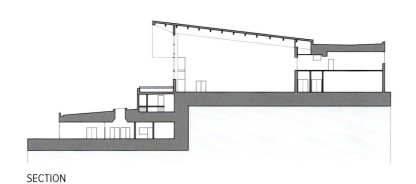

SECTION

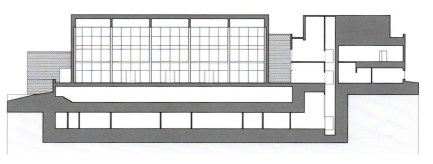

SECTION

FORT DALLES TRAINING CENTER

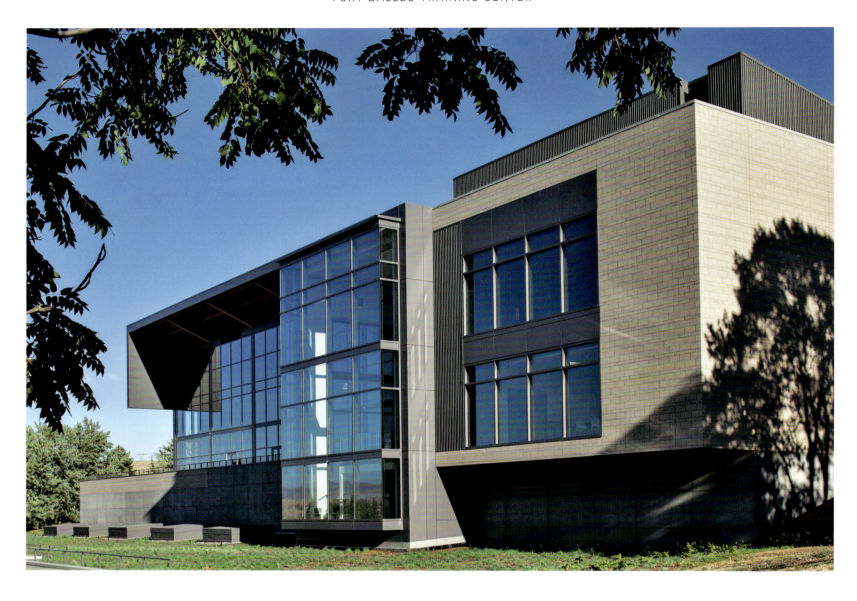

The building needed to be secure for OMD but also open and welcoming enough to serve as a community center, a teaching environment, and a venue able to be rented for public functions.

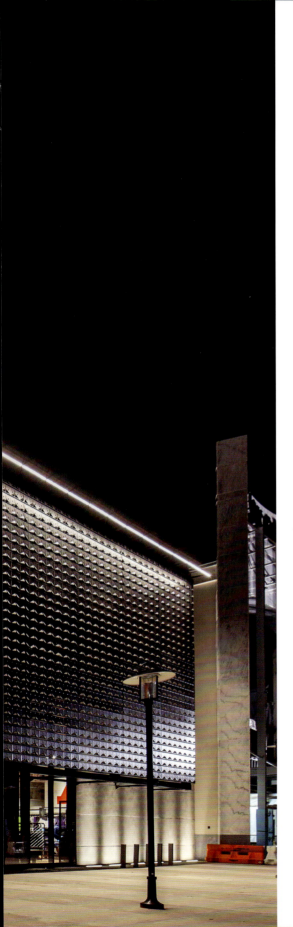

NIKE RETAIL STORES

ATLANTA, GA | CHICAGO, IL | SANTA MONICA, CA | SEATTLE, WA

In the late 1980s Nike began its first cutting edge retail store roll out and introduced to the world "Niketown," which was a combination retail store and product museum. These flagship stores redefined the art of retailing product based upon the development of strong storytelling in support of Nike's growing product lines. Located across the United States and Europe, Niketowns became the front door for introducing the world to the latest cutting-edge Nike footwear and apparel. The store concept was so popular that it became the number one tourist destination in Chicago in the early 1990s.

In 2010, Nike reached out and we began collaborating on an aggressive rebranding program specific to redefining the language and storytelling behind these stores. We began working closely with Nike Retail developing a new architectural language that focused on creating a new language inspired by old field houses, temples for sport and competition. The new stores became a platform for exploration, experimentation and exhibition of their latest product lines. These direct-to-consumer stores catalyzed a connection to the communities they served and built relationships that encouraged sport and activity through data driven curation. Having completed new stores in over two dozen locations, we have been a steadfast partner to Nike's internal design team as they roll out new retail environments across the United States. TVA has facilitated projects in all types of settings, from ground-up flagship stores to interior tenant remodels.

The following pages illustrate a cross section of four of the Nike retail branded stores from across the United States that defined the "Field House" brand language that we implemented in our first store working with Nike Retail Design on the Third Street Mall in Santa Monica which opened in the summer of 2011.

NIKE RETAIL STORES—ATLANTA

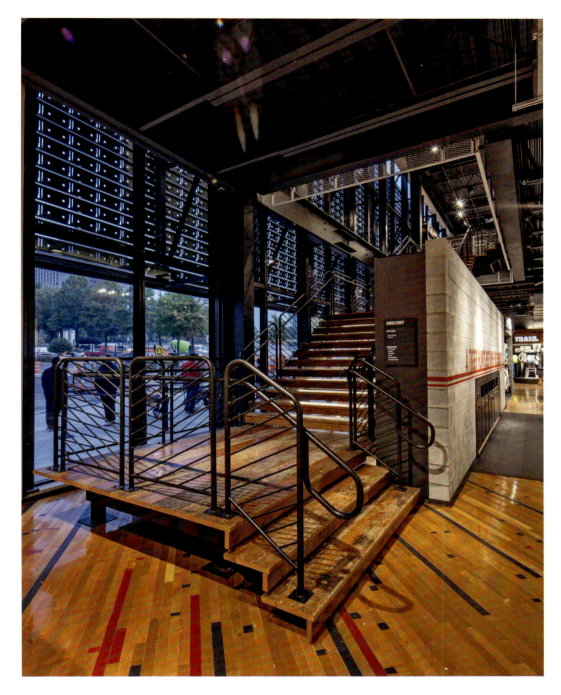

The Nike Retail store in Atlanta features recycled gymnasium floors that speak to the "Field House" brand language. Large open stairs connect the two floors behind a distinctive exterior façade consisting of bent metal panels reminiscent of the waffle pattern at the core of the Nike brand.

NIKE RETAIL STORES—ATLANTA

TVA Architects collaborated with Nike Retail Design to create and develop the "Field House" brand language in the stores, inspired by old field houses, temples for sport and competition.

SECOND-FLOOR PLAN

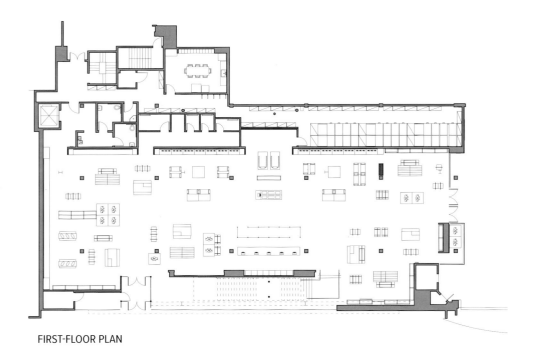

FIRST-FLOOR PLAN

NIKE RETAIL STORES—ATLANTA

The retail space became a platform for exploration, experimentation, and exhibition of Nike's latest product lines.

The first Niketown retail store in Chicago proved to be immensely popular, and was the number one tourist destination in the early 1990s.

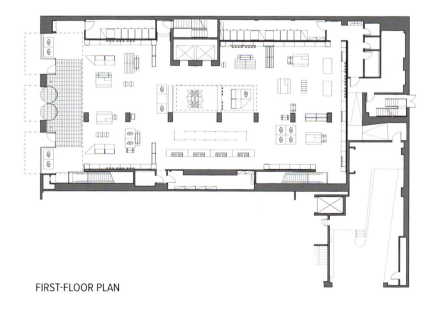

FIRST-FLOOR PLAN

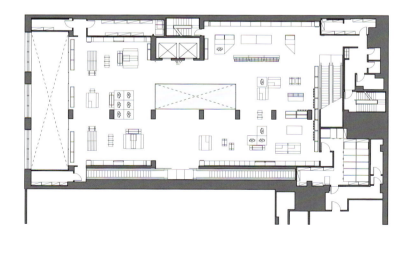

SECOND-FLOOR PLAN

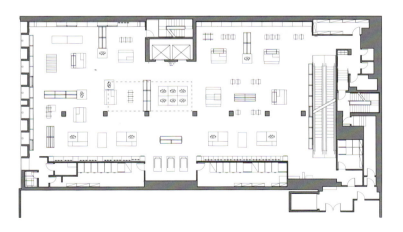

THIRD-FLOOR PLAN

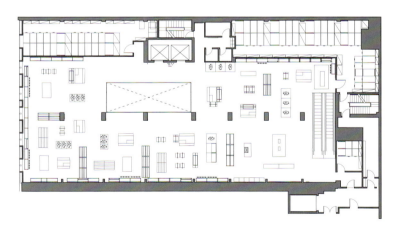

FOURTH-FLOOR PLAN

NIKE RETAIL STORES—SANTA MONICA

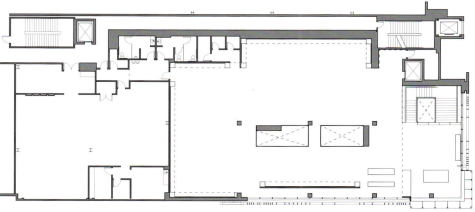

SECOND-FLOOR PLAN

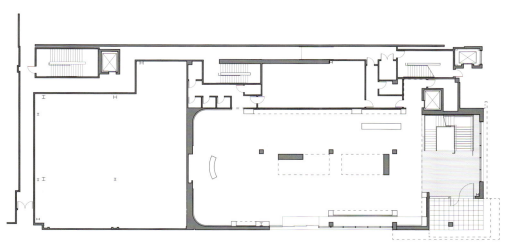

FIRST-FLOOR PLAN

TVA has facilitated projects in all types of settings, from ground-up flagship stores, such as the Santa Monica Nike Retail store, to interior tenant remodels.

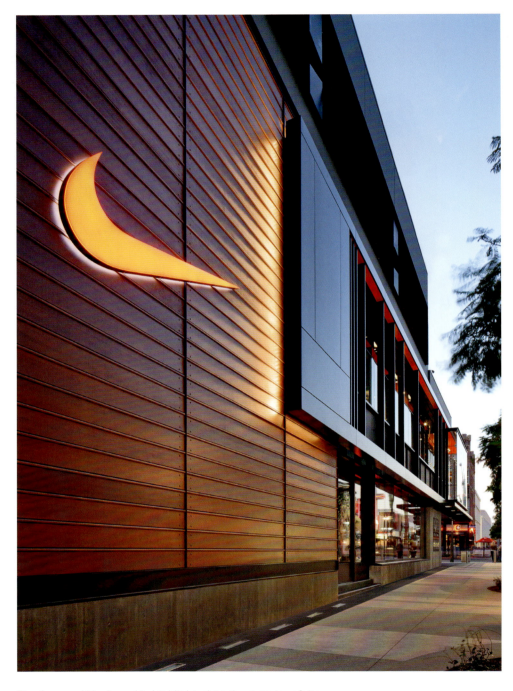

The famous Nike brand is highlighted on the exterior of the Santa Monica Nike Retail store. TVA has been a steadfast partner to Nike's internal design team as they roll out new retail environments across the United States.

The revamped direct-to-consumer stores showcasing the latest Nike products catalyzed a connection to the communities they served and built relationships that encouraged sport and activity.

NIKE RETAIL STORES—SEATTLE

The Nike Retail store in Seattle provides an example of the rebranding program specific to redefining the language and storytelling behind these stores.

NIKE RETAIL STORES—SEATTLE

FIRST-FLOOR PLAN

SECOND-FLOOR PLAN

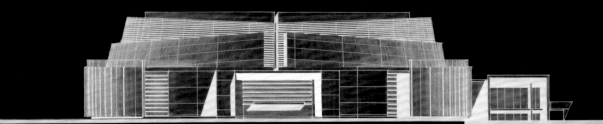

Oregon Arena · East 1" = 20'

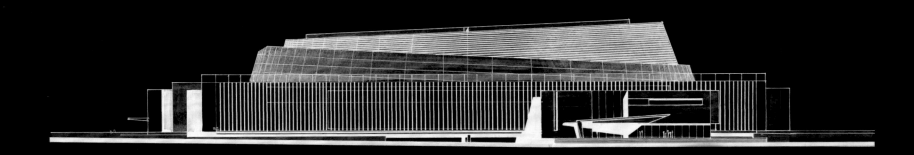

Oregon Arena · North 1" = 20'

& ARTS, SPORTS & CULTURE

SOU PERFORMING ARTS CENTER

ASHLAND, OREGON | 2018 | 58,000 SQ FT

To better support the growing theater program at Southern Oregon University (SOU) and to house the Jefferson Public Radio (JPR) functions on campus, we completed a renovation and new addition to SOU's existing two-story performing arts theater building. A new movement studio and computer lab were added, as well as two new rehearsal studios and upgrading the existing costume shop.

JPR, the regional public broadcasting network for southern Oregon and northern California, has been based on the SOU campus since it first began as a student-run station in the 1960s. The new two-story addition for JPR features a performance space, eight new offices, four "on-air" talk studios, three audiovisual production rooms, support and conference spaces, and open office space. The building supports the original campus master plan through the design of a gracious gallery space that connects the theater program with the JPR program. This gallery is located on what was previously a major pedestrian path cutting through the center of campus. Use of the gallery as an organizing design principal for the building also created an opportunity for all campus visitors to pass through this building, thus putting the art on display and exposing students not currently engaged in these classes to the nationally recognized SOU theater arts program.

The existing theater building was a simple rectangular brick block with punched openings devoid of any windows or visual connection to the SOU campus. Our view was that theater buildings, much like campus union buildings, form the heart of university campuses in that they act as major gathering and meeting spaces for students and the public. Our approach to the renovation was to open the building up through the introduction of large windows that reinforces the geometry and composition of the new addition. Turning the building inside out and maximizing transparency into the key public spaces allowed us to focus that energy back out into the surroundings where the building now behaves like a lantern and a new addition to campus life. The building was reclad in an off-white-colored brick bringing new radiant light to the form and composition of the theater.

SOU PERFORMING ARTS CENTER

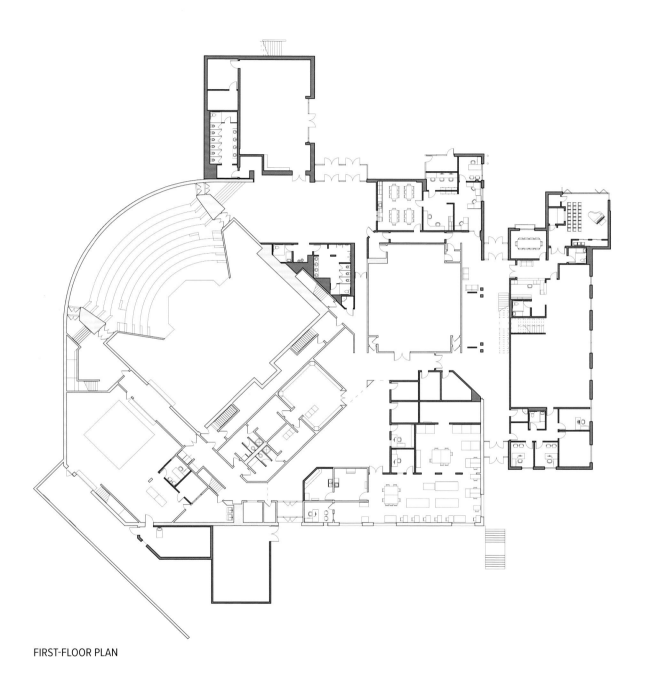

FIRST-FLOOR PLAN

The gallery created an opportunity for all campus visitors to pass through this building, thus putting the art on display and exposing students not currently engaged in these classes to the nationally recognized SOU theater arts program.

The theater building was redesigned to form the heart of the university campus and acts as a major gathering and meeting space for students and the public.

The renovation opened the building up through the introduction of large windows that reinforces the geometry and composition of the new addition.

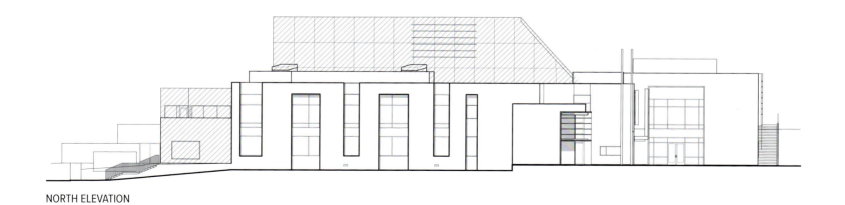

NORTH ELEVATION

MOYER MAUSOLEUM

PORTLAND, OREGON | 2020

In 1984 at the inception of our new firm, I had the great honor of meeting developer Tom Moyer, a Portland icon and leading developer in the Pacific Northwest. I was 30 years old with only four employees in our new office. Tom became the early catalyst behind our firm commissioning us to design small retail projects and multiscreen cinema complexes. Our relationship was based on mutual respect, admiration, and trust. Tom was a man of honor, where a handshake was his contract and his word. He represented the integrity of a generation of businessmen and women long passed that I desperately miss. We were partners and collaborators in pursuit of a common goal focused on design and a successful outcome. Tom was an innovator at heart and a risk-taker unlike most of his peers of his time. I loved Tom and owe much of our success to him and his company TMT Development.

In addition to designing theaters, we designed the Marilyn Moyer Meditation Chapel in honor of Tom's wife. This was followed by our first high-rise, the 27-story Fox Tower located in the heart of downtown Portland. Most recently, I collaborated on the design of a beautiful pocket park with celebrated landscape architect Laurie Olin and ZGF Architects design partner and my mentor Robert Frasca on land donated by Tom to the City of Portland immediately behind the Fox Tower. My last project with Tom was designing the 30-story Park Avenue West Tower, a mixed-use office retail and residential tower next to the Fox Tower, completed in 2016. In 2016, Tom passed away at the age of 96.

One of the great honors of my career was being selected by the Moyer family to design a small family mausoleum as Tom's final resting place, which gave me one more opportunity to honor our friendship and to create a piece of architecture that spoke to simple understated modern elegance that he so admired.

Our trusted relationship continues on with Tom's granddaughter and successor Vanessa Sturgeon as we are currently underway designing a large new office building named Flatworks in Portland in addition to a new hotel for Hilton in Salem, Oregon.

MOYER MAUSOLEUM

The small but elegant family mausoleum was a last opportunity to honor my friendship with Tom Moyer.

MOYER MAUSOLEUM

It was a privilege to create a piece of architecture that spoke to a simple understated modern elegance that Tom Moyer so admired.

SITE PLAN

ANKENY PLAZA PAVILION

PORTLAND, OREGON | 2009 | 2,120 SQ FT

Ankeny Plaza Pavilion, located in Waterfront Park, is a highly adaptable multifaceted public urban space that responds to changing patterns of daily and seasonal use—the realization of a long-term vision for the City of Portland. Portland Saturday Market—an eccentric, beloved open market for artisans, food vendors, and street performers—was scheduled for relocation, which provided an opportunity to create a new home for the market in the park, while also serving as a catalyst for revitalizing the adjacent Skidmore-Old Town Historic District, reconnecting that district to the Willamette River, and creating a new public gathering space. The resulting design successfully balances the wide variety of desired programs, upgrades existing park features and seawall, and introduces an over-water overlook. Interactive water play fountains, a market podium and pavilion, and a stormwater garden resolve continuity issues within the park and create visual linkages between the city grid, Ankeny Plaza, and the riverfront.

Located at the northern portion of Portland's landmark Tom McCall Waterfront Park, the pavilion and plaza, when occupied by the market, provides a canopied, bazaar-like atmosphere to the space. During non-market hours, the plaza expands the waterfront's open space with a combination of interactive elements and access to the water. A new central fountain plaza serves as a poetic interpretive installation with a narrative engraved in the plaza steps that describes Portland's settlement and immigration history. The area's history is also reflected by incorporation of the Ankeny Pump Station, an historic utility building adjacent to the river that had been fenced off for decades. Pavers echo the area's historic cobblestones and define the entry to the waterfront from the historic district.

Our renovation of the park reinforces and reconnects the Skidmore-Old Town Historic District of Portland to the Willamette River, creating a new public gathering space for events and functions while establishing a new home for the Portland Saturday Market.

ANKENY PLAZA PAVILION

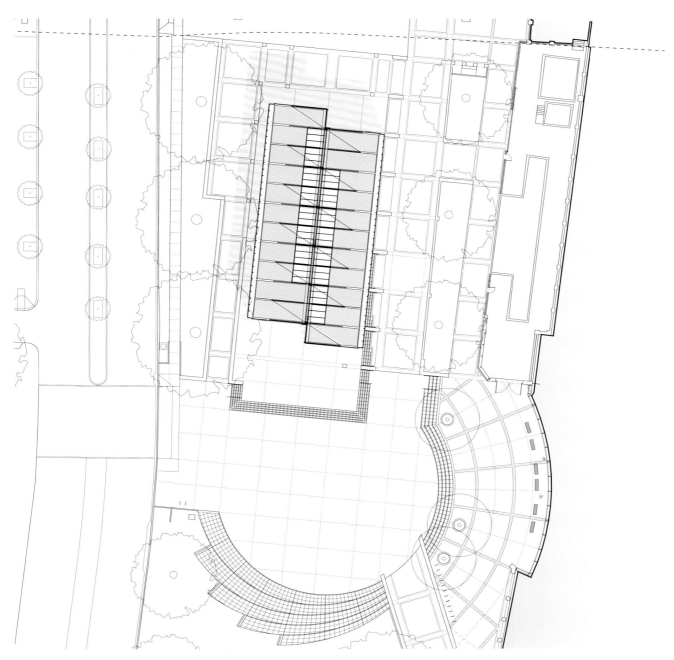

SITE PLAN

The market podium, situated between the Burnside Bridge and the fountain plaza, is raised approximately 3½ feet above the lower plaza to work with the existing oak trees and existing utility vault elevations. The pavilion aligns with the north–south orientation of the riverfront. Reinforced by rows of tall mature specimen oak trees on both sides, it frames views through Burnside Bridge to Waterfront Park. The unique structure comprises a canopy of steel and glass; a roof—64 feet wide, 150 feet long, and 16½ feet high—suspended by rods from a central row of steel columns. It covers the majority of market booths on the podium with wings that resemble the historic fin-shaped awnings that were once common in the historic Skidmore neighborhood.

A significant challenge for the new market podium and plaza was to create interest in the space during non-market hours. The park has an interactive water feature in two different areas. A sophisticated interactive water feature under the pavilion activates the space with water play. After hours, the shelter fountain activates vertical water jets that alternate and react to interruption and interaction. Concrete blocks under the pavilion serve dual roles as utility service points for market stalls and as seat walls.

Outside market season and days of operation, the structure is a multiuse space, adaptable to many different fairs and events that occur regularly in Waterfront Park. When not in use for markets or festivals, the structure becomes a piece of sculpture for the city, fully complementing the park design in which it resides.

DIRECTOR PARK PAVILIONS

PORTLAND, OREGON | 2010 | 750 SQ FT

Director Park was a welcome addition to the urban fabric of downtown Portland, providing high-quality open space for residents, visitors, and shoppers that contributed to the revitalization of the West End. The Park was the vision of Portland developer Tom Moyer who donated the land to the city for the creation of a new central city pocket park that would continue the vision of a necklace of small, half-block parks connecting the North park blocks to the South park blocks. Planning for the design and construction of Director Park involved a citizen steering committee and numerous public involvement opportunities, including presentations, open houses, and workshops. Tom Moyer was my first client when I started TVA Architects in 1984. Tom was a developer with great vision and passion for the future of the City of Portland. I was honored to be awarded multiple design commissions working closely with Tom on the design of Portland landmarks, including Director Park, the Fox Tower, Park Avenue West Tower as well as multiple theaters throughout the Seattle area. The final design concept was the result of a collaborative process involving several design firms including TVA, ZGF Architects, OLIN, and Mayer/Reed, together with the City of Portland Department of Parks and Recreation.

The park was built over a new six-level below-ground parking garage that serves both Fox Tower and Park Avenue West Tower. The plaza above provided the canvas for a composition of structures and spaces that accommodate various functions. As an extension of the parking structures below, TVA designed the small, glassy pavilions to shelter users as they access the elevators to and from the underground parking. The pavilions help define the park edges as well as act as illuminated lanterns in the park at night.

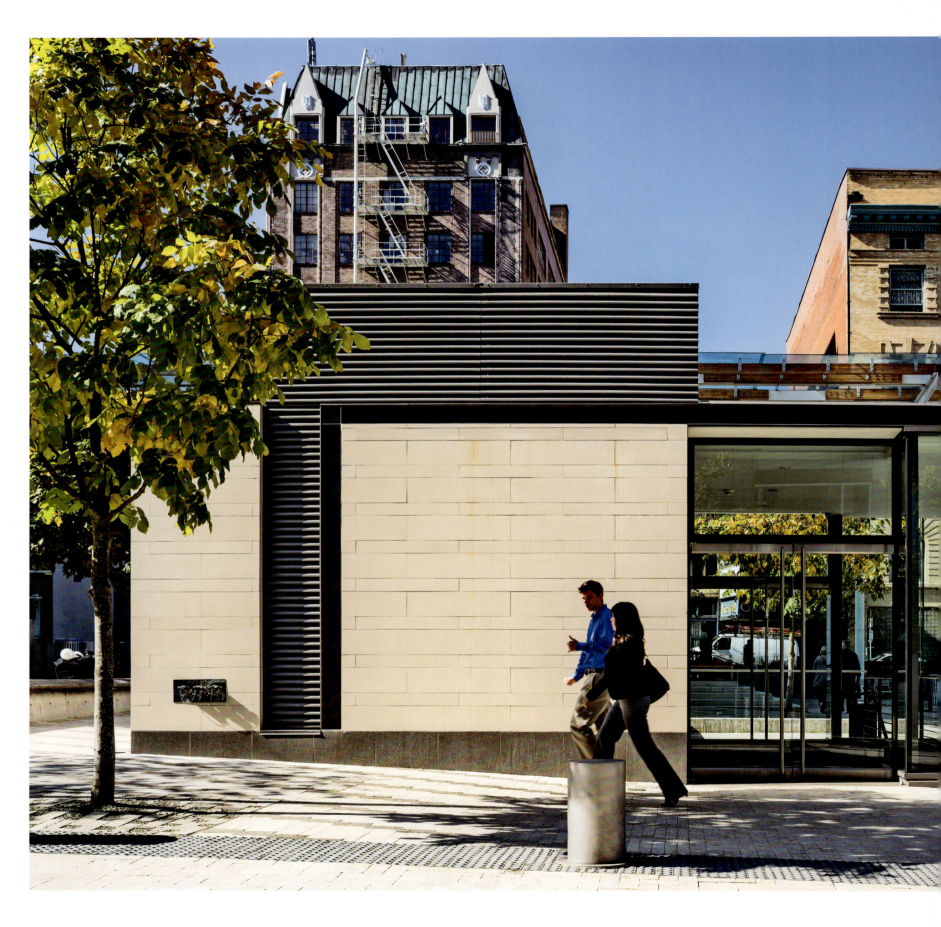

Thompson's small glass pavilions shelter users as they access the elevators to and from the six-level below-grade parking structure designed to support growing retail in the district as well as the new adjacent Park Avenue West Tower to the north.

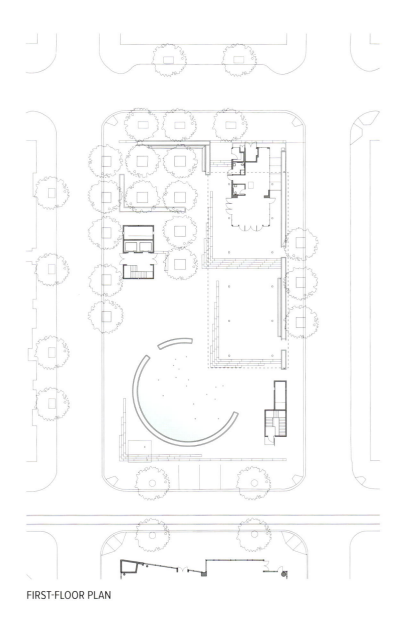

FIRST-FLOOR PLAN

DIRECTOR PARK PAVILIONS

The pavilions help define the park edges as well as act as illuminated lanterns in the park at night.

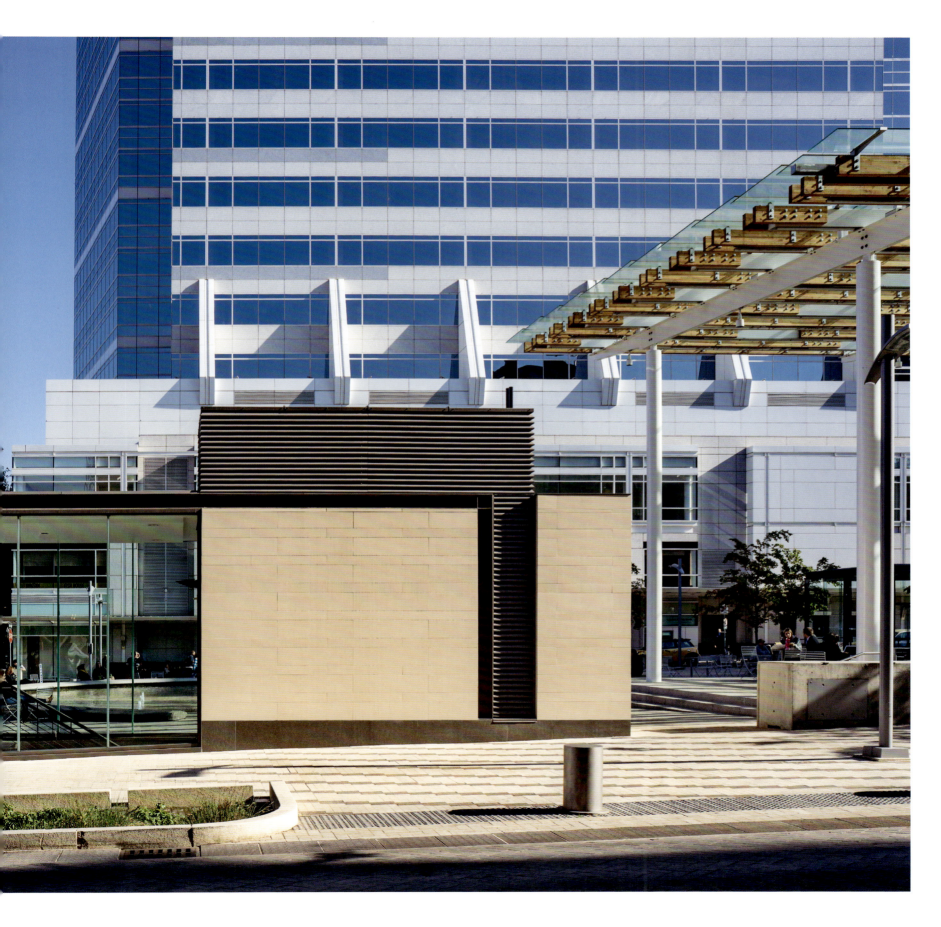

MATTHEW KNIGHT ARENA

EUGENE, OREGON | 2010 | 422,280 SQ FT | LEED GOLD

The Matthew Knight Arena and Ford Alumni Center are located adjacent to one another and are integrated to form a new east gateway to the University of Oregon campus. Providing a first impression of the university's distinct identity, the buildings exemplify the core values of progressive thinking, education, and environmental stewardship of the institution. We worked with the State of Oregon SEED program to achieve a 20 percent energy reduction below code for both the arena and Alumni Center.

Hosting the start of the 2010 basketball season, the arena is a world-class "theater for basketball" that respectfully acknowledges the legend of the university's revered "Mac" Court which it replaced and its historic role in collegiate athletics, while addressing present-day needs for safety, modern amenities, and sustainability. Encompassing 422,280 square feet and accommodating 12,500 seats, the LEED Gold—targeted six-level building is divided into an event level, mezzanine, practice facility, main concourse, balcony seating, mechanical fan room, and catwalk, allowing access to spotlight platforms, rigging grid, and the scoreboard platform. The event floor has an area of 29,000 square feet when retractable seating is stored in place. A portable basketball floor permitting two full sideways basketball courts for practices and camps is adjacent to the playing court.

Large enough to host first- and second-round games in the NCAA Tournament and to accommodate a growing community, the new facility also allows more flexibility for non-basketball events such as concerts and family shows. The design reflects an effort to share the excitement of the arena activities with the outside world through the use of transparent materials, and allowing internal circulation to be open to both the arena and concourses throughout. In addition, the facility features luxury suites low in the seating bowl that place suite holders closer to the action while providing seclusion for private entertainment.

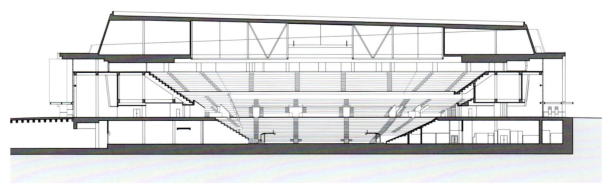

SECTION

Adjacent to the arena is the LEED Gold—targeted Ford Alumni Center building. The four-story, 62,700-square-foot building functions as a welcome center for prospective students, returning alumni and campus visitors, and provides event and gathering space. It also functions as a reception center for arena activities, while the outdoor plaza areas become vibrant spaces when events are held at the arena. The Ford Alumni Center is constructed on top of an underground parking structure with 377 below-ground parking stalls accommodating arena events, as well as student parking and special university functions. The garage has direct elevator access leading to the main north entry plaza serving both buildings.

The Matthew Knight Arena and Ford Alumni Center are located adjacent to one another and are integrated to form a new east gateway to the University of Oregon campus.

The arena is a world-class "theater for basketball" that also allows more flexibility for non-basketball events such as concerts and family shows.

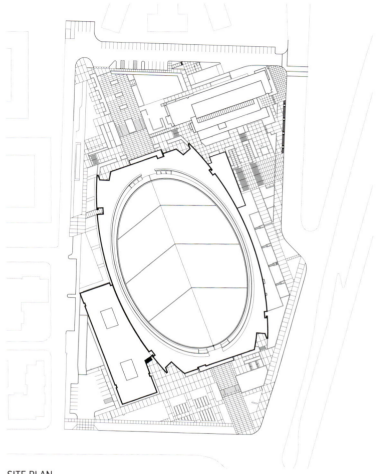

SITE PLAN

The arena is located adjacent to the Ford Alumni Center, and the outdoor plaza areas become vibrant spaces when events are held at the arena.

The use of transparent materials reflects an effort to share the excitement of the arena activities with the outside world. Internal circulation is open to both the arena and concourses throughout.

MATTHEW KNIGHT ARENA

Providing a first impression of the university's distinct identity, the building exemplifies the core values of the institution while addressing present-day needs for safety, modern amenities, and sustainability.

227

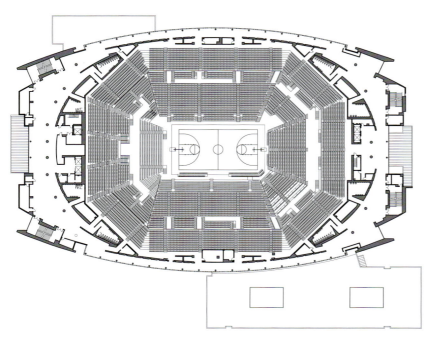

FOURTH-FLOOR PLAN

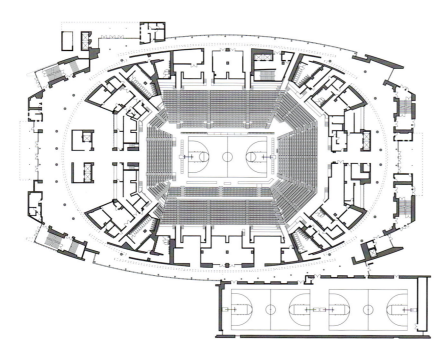

FIRST-FLOOR PLAN

COACHES OFFICE MKA

EUGENE, OREGON | 2020

In 2018, nine years after designing the Matthew Knight Arena, TVA was commissioned to design a new three-story addition to the arena that would facilitate coaching offices for men and women's basketball as well as women's volleyball. Locating the coaching offices on-site gives the student athletes the ability to meet coaches in the same building where they train, allowing them the ability to streamline communication with staff in a space dedicated to mentorship and training. The addition is located at the east end of the existing practice courts, where each floor is designed around a central open spine. This allows views from the coach's office over the practice courts, as well as providing branding and storytelling space speaking to the history of Oregon Basketball and Volleyball. The architecture of the new addition has been carefully designed to honor and respect the existing arena building specific to massing and form as well as consistency in materials.

COACHES OFFICE MKA

THIRD-FLOOR PLAN

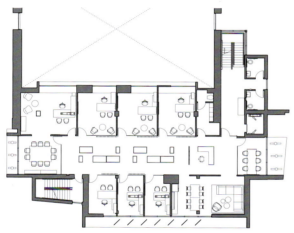

SECOND-FLOOR PLAN

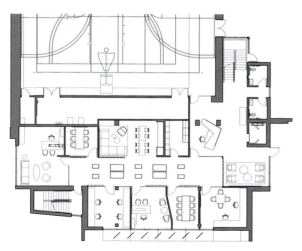

FIRST-FLOOR PLAN

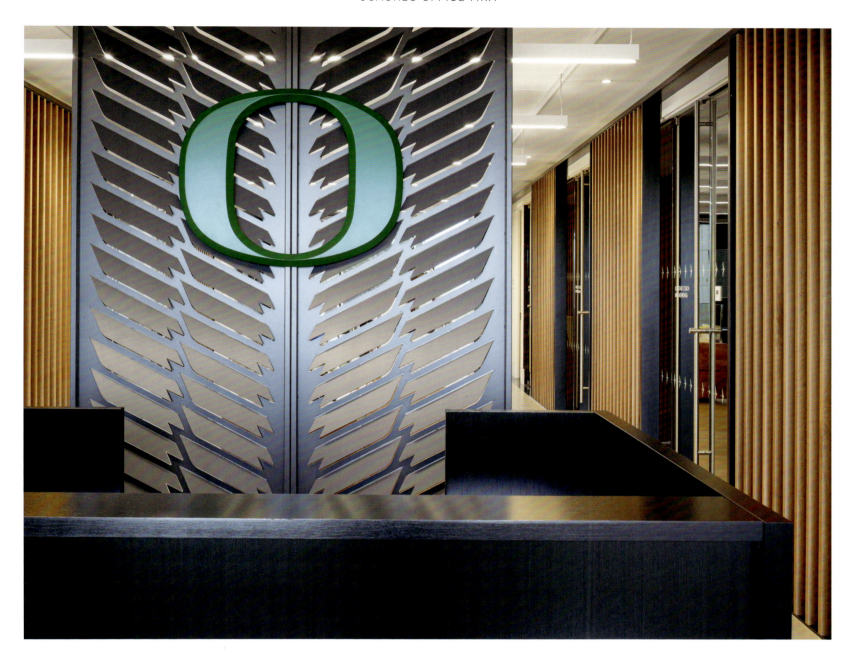

The new addition provides branding and storytelling space speaking to the history of Oregon Basketball and Volleyball.

The addition is located at the east end of the existing practice courts, where each floor is designed around a central open spine, allowing views from the coach's office over the practice courts.

NIKE WORLD HEADQUARTERS

BEAVERTON, OREGON | SOUTH CAMPUS 1990; NORTH CAMPUS 2001

My relationship with Nike began in the spring of 1987 when we were asked to compete in a national competition to design a new corporate headquarters for what was at that time a young, growing footwear and apparel company based in Portland, Oregon.

At that time, Nike employed roughly 700 people and was housed in over 21 separate locations throughout the Portland area. Consolidation, flexibility, and brand identity were high priorities outlined as key goals in the design narrative. The year 1987 was pivotal for Nike with Michael Jordan's raise, the introduction of the Nike Air Max and the "JUST DO IT" advertising campaign taking flight resulting in sales doubling annually for a number of years to come. Our firm at the time was only three years old and we were just gaining traction and visibility in the architectural community through winning design awards for our work and being published in numerous architectural trade journals. That fall following the design presentations Nike co-founder Mr Knight notified us that we had been selected as the winning entry and to begin work immediately. For us the new headquarters was far more than simply providing office space for a growing young company. Our goal was to design a new innovative workplace environment that spoke to a corporate community that would foster, support, and nurture collaboration, camaraderie, and creativity dialogue; a new home designed around sports, athletic performance, sports history, and authenticity; a world that would inspire young designers creating new innovative products from footwear to apparel and equipment. It was essential that the new campus spoke to and built on Nike's culture and the company brand.

NIKE WORLD HEADQUARTERS—SOUTH CAMPUS

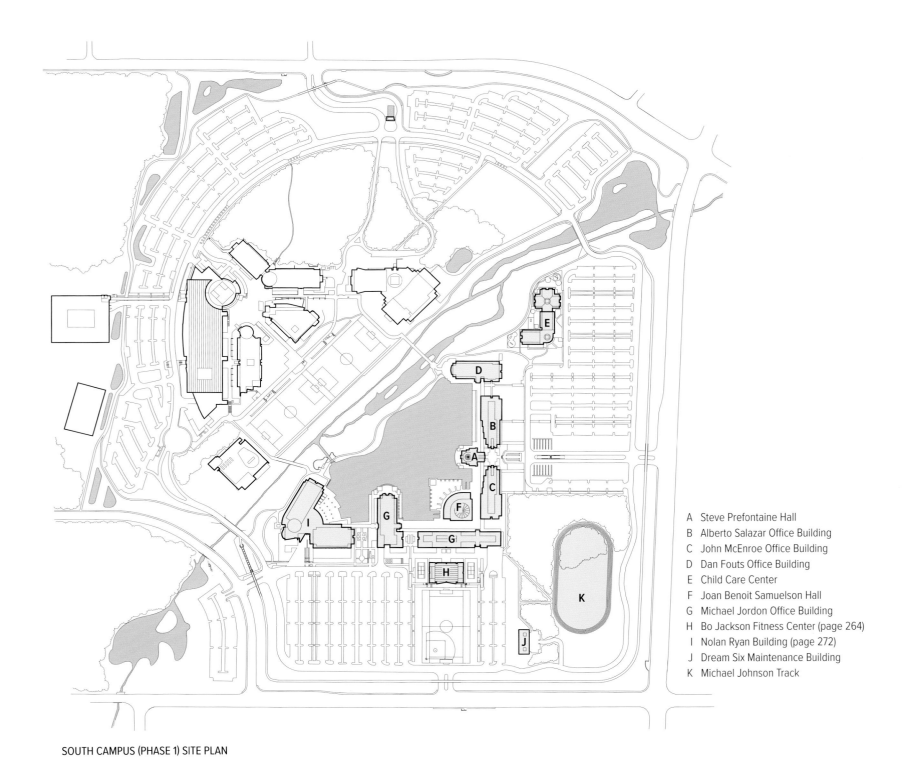

A Steve Prefontaine Hall
B Alberto Salazar Office Building
C John McEnroe Office Building
D Dan Fouts Office Building
E Child Care Center
F Joan Benoit Samuelson Hall
G Michael Jordon Office Building
H Bo Jackson Fitness Center (page 264)
I Nolan Ryan Building (page 272)
J Dream Six Maintenance Building
K Michael Johnson Track

SOUTH CAMPUS (PHASE 1) SITE PLAN

NIKE WORLD HEADQUARTERS—SOUTH CAMPUS

The design program for the 1987 first phase dubbed the South Campus called for 1,030,000 square feet to be located in ten new buildings on 87 acres. The directive included five new office buildings consisting of flexible open creative workspace, a new product design center, a central reception building that would become the new front door to Nike and support both company as well as public events with displays that spoke to the company's history and culture. Additionally the program called for a company daycare center in addition to a large commons building that would act as the campus living room and social center supported by the campus cafeteria and separate sports bar. At the heart of the master plan, a new seven-acre lake became the key organizing element that shaped the design and land plan for the buildings. A major athletics facility containing basketball, aerobics, weight rooms, racquetball courts, and an international-sized soccer field anchored the south side of the campus and was placed on axis to the South Campus vehicular entry. The Nolan Ryan building, which housed all Nike apparel design, anchored the west edge of the campus while the east edge was home to a new 400-meter, six-lane running track.

Phase 1 of the Nike World Headquarters was completed and opened in the fall of 1990. Between 1990 and 1995, Nike experienced tremendous industry growth becoming the leading footwear and apparel company in the world. With that growth in sales, new employee recruitment ballooned to over 5,000 and Nike was once again expanding into off-campus lease space throughout the city. In the fall of 1995, Nike's Board of Directors approved the second phase expansion of the campus consisting of 1.5 million square feet to be located adjacent to the South Campus on 110 acres. The program called for eight new buildings housing office and design studios, a new footwear and apparel design center, a second major athletics club, a second daycare center as well as a major new conference center designed to support all campus meetings and events, including a 900-seat performing arts theater. Following a limited design competition TVA was once again selected by Nike as the architect for the new North Campus expansion.

NIKE WORLD HEADQUARTERS—SOUTH CAMPUS

At the heart of the master plan, a new seven-acre lake became the key organizing element that shaped the design and land plan for the buildings.

The Nike campus was designed to be a new and innovative workplace environment that spoke to and built on Nike's culture and the company brand.

NIKE WORLD HEADQUARTERS—NORTH CAMPUS

Like the first phase, the North Campus is a sympathetic response to the natural landscape elements and conditions that comprise the site. Existing tree groves, topography, wetlands, and views informed the solution creating a scheme that united both the built and the natural environments. The plan presents an orthogonal response to the South Campus, set up by the orientation of two end-to-end international-sized soccer fields placed in existing meadows adjacent to a year-round creek that bisects the campus plan. Positioning the fields in existing meadows strengthened the heart of the campus as a complement to the lake, creating a major visual focus as well as a transitional buffer between the first and second phases. To reinforce the athletics fields, the new athletics center as well as the campus conferencing center flank the ends of the fields like bookends giving a sense of containment and enclosure. Rooms created by existing tree groves northwest of the meadows became logical building sites, with the trees acting as a veil obscuring views to and from the South Campus. The use of wooded edges to divide the campus into definable rooms or zones adds richness and layering to the campus experience.

Highly detailed pedestrian streets are branded with large colorful graphic banners that reference sports history and leading athletes who endorse Nike products.

NIKE WORLD HEADQUARTERS—NORTH CAMPUS

Each new building on campus, such as the Mia Hamm Design Center, was celebrated with the name of an elite world-renowned athlete who elevated their sport to new heights and who became a global ambassador representing the Nike brand.

The overall design is a sympathetic response to the natural landscape elements and conditions that comprise the site.

NIKE WORLD HEADQUARTERS—NORTH CAMPUS

The Nike campus was designed around sports, athletic performance, sports history, and authenticity, a world that would inspire young designers creating new and innovative products for the brand from footwear to apparel and equipment.

NIKE WORLD HEADQUARTERS—NORTH CAMPUS

The Ken Griffey Jr. Office Building reinforces the architectural language used in all North Campus buildings, creating a village of buildings that speaks to a common unified architecture. The Walker Street entry is framed by an overhead running bridge creating a portal and gateway entry into the North Campus. A dramatic 200-foot-long water feature designed by renowned landscape architect Robert Murase celebrates arrival into the Nike World Headquarters while speaking to the natural beauty of the Pacific Northwest.

BO JACKSON FITNESS CENTER

NIKE WORLD HEADQUARTERS | BEAVERTON, OREGON | 1989 | 53,200 SQ FT

Occupying a prominent location at the heart of the first phase of the 87-acre Nike World Headquarters campus, the Bo Jackson Fitness Center was designed to demonstrate the essence of Nike to the world. The large center became the heart of the original campus supporting employee intermural and fitness.

The primary south-facing public façade of the building is aligned on axis with an expansive international-sized soccer field, creating the visual foreground to the building as employees and visitors enter onto the campus while passing under the Jenkins Street Bridge, all contributing together to make a major statement about Nike's corporate roots. At night the glazed basketball pavilion acts as an illuminated "stage" highlighting competitive athletics and Nike culture to the public. The sports center has been layered horizontally with lockers, showers, sauna and steam rooms, the Nike-tykes center as well as the Fitness Institute, all programmed on the first floor, forming a strong base for the building. The second floor contains aerobic, weight and circuit training rooms, meeting rooms, juice bar, and lounge. The lounge acts as one of the living rooms or social centers on the campus in addition to the Joan Benoit Samuelson Hall, Mia Hamm Design Center, and the Tiger Woods Conference Center. These spaces foster casual interaction among the employees where dialog about Nike product development can occur as well, promoting company communication and social interaction. Level three forms the top floor and houses the Nike basketball courts in a glass pavilion that retails the energy and competitive play of Nike employees and visiting NBA players who are on campus warming up prior to evening games with the Portland Trailblazers. Four racquetball courts form solid "bookends" to the transparent gymnasium and suspended running track. In contrast to most gymnasium spaces, Nike desired a facility with as much natural daylight as possible to replicate sandlot athletics and the quintessential pick-up game in the park.

BO JACKSON FITNESS CENTER

The primary public façade of the building is aligned on axis with an expansive international-sized soccer field, creating the visual foreground to the building as employees and visitors enter onto the campus and contributing to make a major statement about Nike's corporate roots.

The Nike basketball courts are housed in a glass pavilion that retails the energy and competitive play of Nike employees and visiting NBA players who are on campus warming up prior to evening games with the Portland Trailblazers.

BO JACKSON FITNESS CENTER

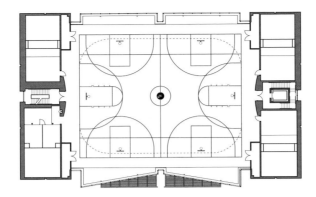

THIRD-FLOOR PLAN

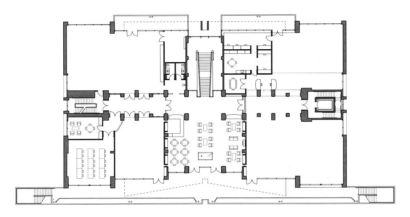

SECOND-FLOOR PLAN

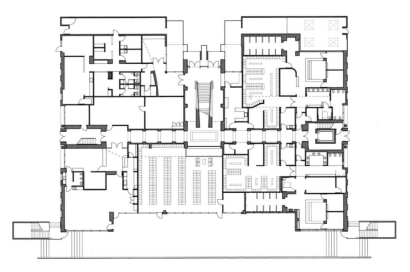

FIRST-FLOOR PLAN

NOLAN RYAN BUILDING

NIKE WORLD HEADQUARTERS | BEAVERTON, OREGON | 1993 | 220,000 SQ FT

Phase 2 of the Nike World Headquarters consists of the development of two office building wings linked around a two-story common entry/reception center that acts as a public hub, and contains a conference space, an employment center, and retail display space. The four-story, 220,000-square-foot building was home to Nike's apparel design divisions, as well as international administration, before all design was moved to the new Mia Hamm Design Center in 2000. Clad in white precast concrete and composite metal panels, the building speaks to a simplistic sculptural elegance reinforcing the architectural language of the campus.

Located on the western end of the campus, the building plays a key role in completing and containing the lake, and is connected to the first phase through an extension of the covered arcade. It provides space for 650 employees in a flexible open office space that allows for Nike's continued growth and never-ending change.

Interior spaces have been designed using light maple paneling and black slate as accents, creating a warmth and richness to the work environment and a neutral color palette as the backdrop to apparel product development. Movable custom workstations have been designed to allow for maximum flexibility in the creation of working neighborhoods that house individual product category groups.

At the center of each office wing, four-story, open-stair atriums provide vertical circulation and visual connection between the floors and act as paths of communication. Flanking the atriums in each building are conference rooms, restrooms, and copier/coffee stations, creating clarity and continuity between the buildings.

Clad in white precast concrete and composite metal panels, the building speaks to a simplistic sculptural elegance reinforcing the architectural language of the campus.

At the center of each office wing, four-story, open-stair atriums provide vertical circulation and visual connection between the floors and act as paths of communication.

Interior spaces have been designed using light maple paneling and black slate as accents, creating a warmth and richness to the work environment and a neutral color palette as the backdrop to apparel product development.

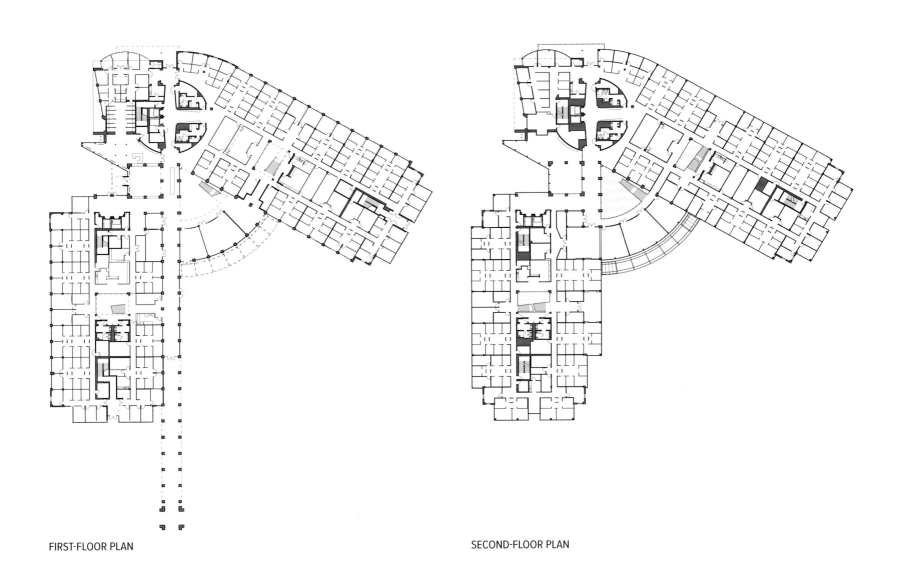

FIRST-FLOOR PLAN

SECOND-FLOOR PLAN

NOLAN RYAN BUILDING

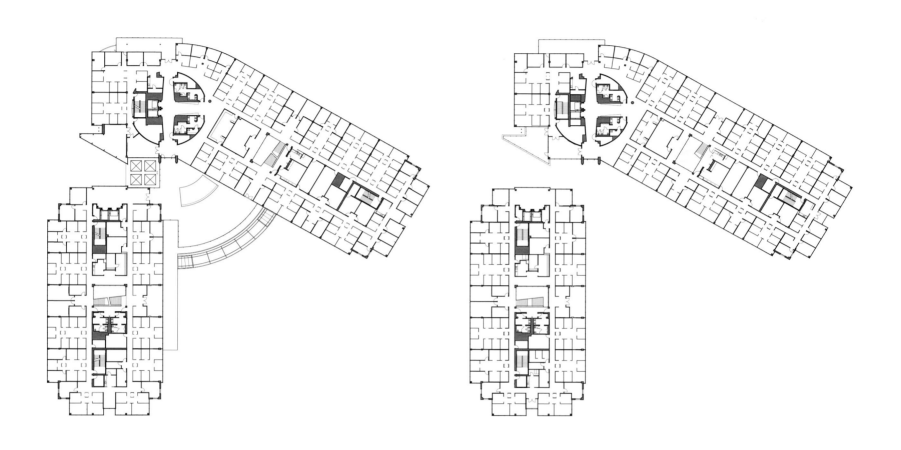

THIRD-FLOOR PLAN

FOURTH-FLOOR PLAN

JERRY RICE BUILDING

NIKE WORLD HEADQUARTERS | BEAVERTON, OREGON | 1999 | 225,000 SQ FT

The Jerry Rice Building became the first of three new office buildings in the Nike North Campus expansion that we started designing in the fall of 1995. Unlike the first phase where we created a seven-acre lake as the key organizing element to the land plan, we used Phase 2 as an opportunity to develop a more urban solution focusing the new six-building scheme around a town square as a way of amplifying employee connection and interaction. Building entries, cafés, outdoor seating and dining as well, as all campus functions occupy the square throughout the year, and introduces another major social interactive hub to campus life.

The Jerry Rice Building comprises two four-story office wings that hinge around a central radial entry lobby. The building creates a strong edge along the north side of the square creating containment while facilitating employee movement as one moves from the South Campus through the North Campus to parking beyond. In the new North Campus we introduced a workplace planning concept we defined as "neighborhoods," which consisted of seven open workstations and one private office framing an open flexible work bay enabling user groups the flexibility of using that area as they choose to create a workplace that best supported their teams and culture. Staying consistent with the architectural language and material palette of buildings on campus, white precast concrete coupled with white composite metal panels make up the exterior cladding materials creating a neutral backdrop that is elegant and timeless.

JERRY RICE BUILDING

Staying consistent with the architectural language and material palette of buildings on campus, white precast concrete coupled with white composite metal panels make up the exterior cladding materials creating a neutral backdrop that is elegant and timeless.

JERRY RICE BUILDING

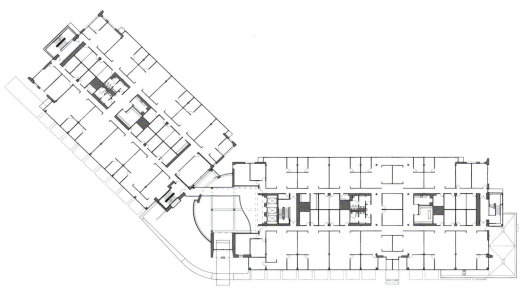

FOURTH-FLOOR PLAN

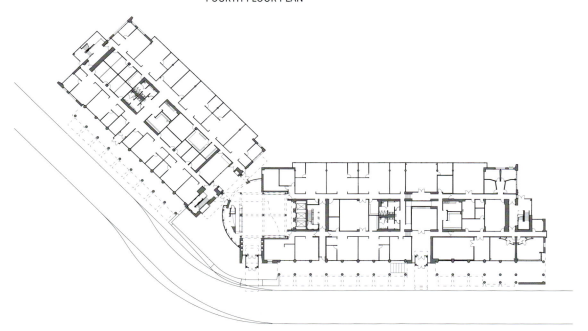

FIRST-FLOOR PLAN

The building comprises two four-story office wings that hinge around a central radial entry lobby.

The Jerry Rice Building anchors the north edge of the campus creating containment and a framework that gives definition to the campus "town square." Buildings are linked with covered walkways that provide weather protection as employees move throughout the campus. History plaques adorn the covered walkways celebrating the achievements of Nike athletes and key individuals who have played a major role in representing the Nike brand both on and off the field.

NIKE GATEHOUSE

NIKE WORLD HEADQUARTERS | BEAVERTON, OREGON | 1998 | 400 SQ FT

The Nike Gatehouse is a 400-square-foot reception center that welcomes visitors to the Nike North Campus. While security is strict and control important, it is critical that visitors and employees feel welcomed. The reception center is also the first building one comes upon while entering the campus.

The visitor enters the campus at the low point of the site and proceeds a short distance to the top of a hill along a heavily landscaped split-entry drive. On the approach to the gatehouse a large reflecting basin creates the foreground to the building and acts as a mirror reflecting the sky and adjacent trees. The plan allows security personnel access to visitors approaching and leaving the campus.

The simplicity of the plan is reflected in the building elevations where long, sleek aluminum overhangs provide sun protection cantilevering off the precast skin of the main building. The building is capped with a low-slung barrel roof that allows for soft, indirect light in the day yet glows with indirect lighting reflecting off maple paneled ceilings.

White precast panels and white aluminum paneled sunshades and roofing comprise the exterior material palette. The interiors consist of maple casework and maple-paneled curved ceilings with stone-clad flooring.

The Nike Gatehouse is designed as a welcome center greeting visitors and employees to the campus. The small jewel box is an introduction to the architectural language that comprises the campus buildings and speaks to an understated modern elegance woven into the natural landscape inherent of the Pacific Northwest.

NIKE GATEHOUSE

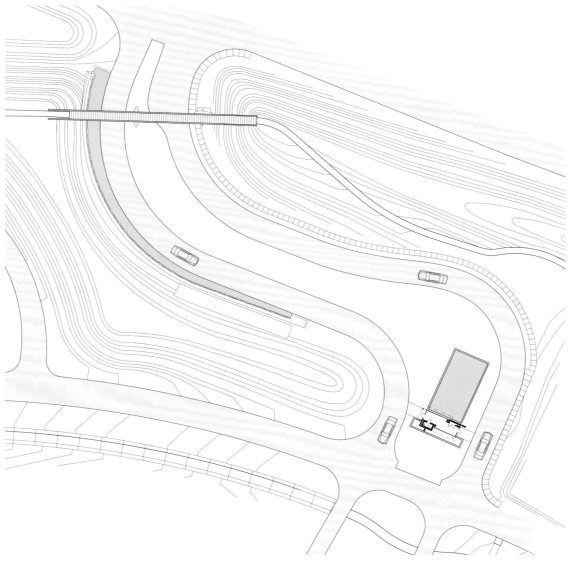

SITE PLAN

Entry to the campus is along a heavily landscaped split-entry drive. On the approach to the gatehouse a large reflecting basin creates the foreground to the building and acts as a mirror reflecting the sky and adjacent trees.

THE PARK

NIKE WORLD HEADQUARTERS | BEAVERTON, OREGON | 2000 | 440,500 SQ FT

During Nike's explosive growth that occurred during the late 1990s and with the North Campus expansion well underway it became clear that land was the one commodity that could not be manufactured and that future campus growth over the coming decades would be limited by the amount of available land. Phase 1 and 2 of the campus consisted primarily of surface parking for 5,000 cars as well as buildings that were held to four stories as directed by Nike's senior management. In an effort to deal with the growing demand for on-site parking as well as a desire to conserve land we designed a seven-story parking garage located on the western edge of campus as a part of the second phase that would support 750 cars. To weave the garage into the language of the campus buildings we decided to use it as a major branding opportunity, a billboard that would celebrate the great sporting venues and ballparks throughout the world. Using an inkjet process on light translucent perforated film we created a collage consisting of ballparks (like The Boston Garden, Solders Field in Chicago, and Hayward Field in Eugene, Oregon, to name just a few) to create a colorful dynamic statement that spoke to sports and the Nike culture. At night, the five-story wall of scrim is illuminated, turning the "mundane" garage into a cultural statement that references the culture of sports, competition, innovation, and athletics.

THE PARK

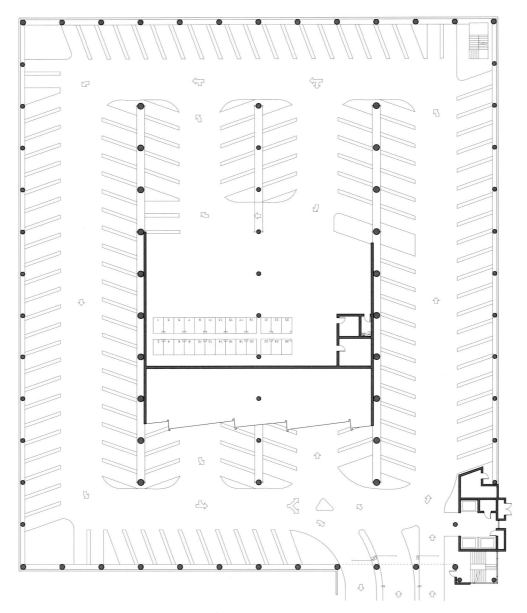

FIRST-FLOOR PLAN

Clad in white precast panels and wrapped in a translucent scrim fabric adorned with images of world-famous ball parks, The Park consolidates 750 cars into a seven-story garage, preserving valuable real estate for future campus expansions.

MIA HAMM DESIGN CENTER

NIKE WORLD HEADQUARTERS | BEAVERTON, OREGON | 2000 | 449,000 SQ FT

The Mia Hamm Design Center became the largest building on the Nike site when completed. In the initial programming stages I spent time with Nike co-founder Phil Knight who emphasized that the design center should be a dynamic piece of architecture but more importantly it needed to function as a flexible environment that could accommodate constant change, and as such it needed to act as a neutral space designed with total flexibility to change with the never-ending needs of the Nike product design teams. It needed to support, not compete. As Nike was doubling in size annually, the infrastructure to support the enormous growth was essential for Nike to sustain its role as the largest footwear and apparel company in the world. The North Campus expansion of the Nike World Headquarters represented a doubling in area of the existing original South Campus, and the Mia Hamm building became the center for creative innovation of new products.

Nike wanted to consolidate all its product designers into a single location where they could co-exist, collaborate, interact, and flex, forming a creative think tank shared across all brands. The lowest level of the building caters to support product development and modeling in addition to shipping, receiving, and storage. Level two forms the main floor, and opens out to the complex's square and adjacent building. Two branded restaurants at the northern end provide food service and dining for employees in large, open cafés as well as a more intimate coffee bar. The design center is located at the heart of the North Campus site and is the centerpiece of the seven-building expansion master plan. During fair weather, the cafés spill out onto the central precinct square through large operable sliding doors. As technology has developed employees now enjoy the luxury of being able to work remotely at any location across the campus elevating the importance of these community spaces to new levels. Level two focuses on product testing and development while levels three and four are reserved for product design. The central bays of level three are defined by large, open industrial warehouse spaces focused on flexibility and light, creating dramatic workplace environments for Nike designers to continue the innovative process of creating state-of-the-art sports and fitness products.

MIA HAMM DESIGN CENTER

The Mia Hamm Design Center was the largest building on campus when completed in 2000. It was the design center for Nike's footwear and apparel development as well as product testing. The north end of the building houses campus amenity spaces, including two cafés, meeting and conferencing spaces as well as the campus library.

MIA HAMM DESIGN CENTER

During fair weather, the cafés spill out onto the central precinct square through large operable sliding doors.

The central bays of level three are defined by large, open industrial warehouse spaces focused on flexibility and light, creating dramatic workplace environments for Nike designers.

MIA HAMM DESIGN CENTER

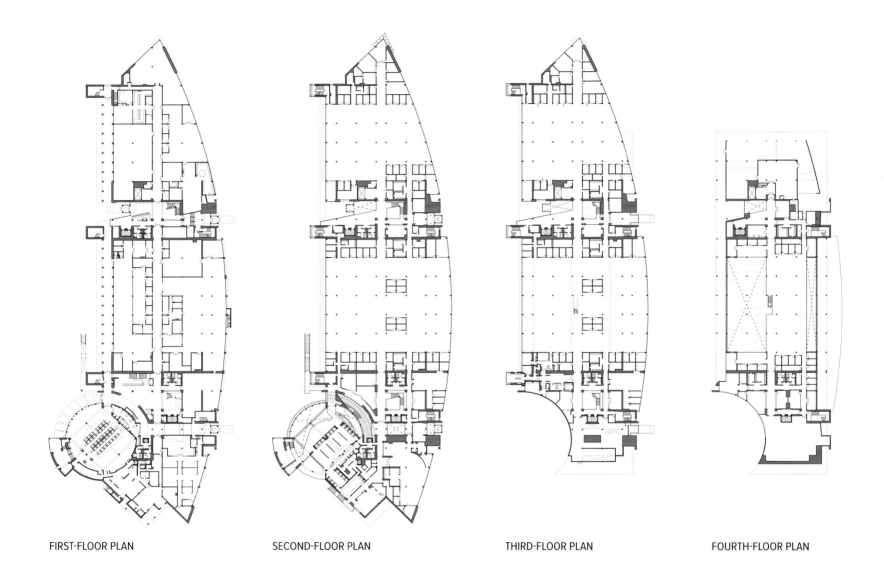

FIRST-FLOOR PLAN

SECOND-FLOOR PLAN

THIRD-FLOOR PLAN

FOURTH-FLOOR PLAN

The Mia Hamm building became the center for creative innovation of new products and needed to act as a neutral space designed with total flexibility to change according to Nike's future needs.

MIA HAMM DESIGN CENTER

TIGER WOODS CONFERENCE CENTER

BEAVERTON, OREGON | 2001 | 145,000 SQ FT

Named for the PGA legend, the Tiger Woods Conference Center at the Nike World Headquarters was designed as a direct response to the company's explosive growth and increasing demands for flexible on-campus showroom and meeting space. The 145,000-square-foot, two-story facility joins 19 existing Thompson-designed buildings at the Nike corporate location, occupying a pivotal site within a four-acre wooded area on campus.

The center will act as the new public front door to Nike and the campus and will be available to the public for select events, including the Oregon Sports Award, annual Nike Board, and Public Share Holder meetings as well as notable charity events. Accessed from the north off of Walker Road, visitors and employees enter the campus passing under one of four branded Nike running bridges and proceed along a 150-foot-long basalt stone water wall before passing through a large beautiful grove of trees to arrive at the front door of the Tiger Woods Conference Center.

Designed to accommodate large quarterly sales meetings, as well as ongoing campus events, the center is the new heart of the campus, the social center that facilitates the large demand for major product presentations, all campus employee gatherings, theatrical presentations, as well as small and large catered meetings with sophisticated audiovisual needs. Large banquet facilities designed to accommodate seating for 650 people are located at the south end of the building with direct access to an outdoor dining space that sits on axis to two international-sized soccer fields. The building design pivots around a large two-story glazed atrium that forms the lobby of the building from which heavily branded smaller breakout seating areas occur, displaying golf memorabilia as well as artifacts relating to the Tiger Woods story. Adjacent to the lobby rotunda is the entry to The Stanford, a 750-seat, two-level performing arts center equipped with state-of-the-art audiovisual technology geared for high-level presentations and quarterly sales meetings. With over 28 separate showrooms and a varied range of meeting rooms, flexibility was key to the design. Level two includes 18 meeting rooms and administration space.

The Tiger Woods Center acts as the public front door to the campus containing Nike's showrooms and event space in addition to The Stanford, a 750-seat performing arts auditorium for large campus events as well as public gatherings.

TIGER WOODS CONFERENCE CENTER

TIGER WOODS CONFERENCE CENTER

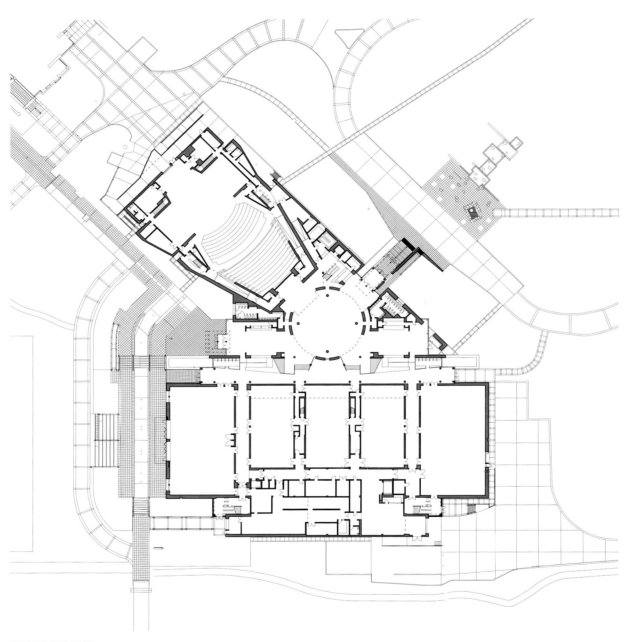

FIRST-FLOOR PLAN

The Stanford is a 750-seat, two-level performing arts center equipped with state-of-the-art audiovisual technology geared for high-level presentations and quarterly sales meetings. Small breakout seating areas display golf memorabilia as well as artifacts relating to the Tiger Woods story.

NIKE SPORTS PERFORMANCE CENTER

NIKE WORLD HEADQUARTERS | BEAVERTON, OREGON | 2001 | 75,000 SQ FT

The Nike Sports Performance Center is a leading state-of-the-art athletics and training center located on the campus of the Nike World Headquarters. It is the second major fitness center we designed on campus for the exclusive use of Nike employees and their families. The program specifically aimed to expand on the provision of new sports facilities not included in the Bo Jackson Fitness Center, originally designed as a part of the first phase of the Nike complex.

An 11-lane, 25-meter (82-foot) pool, a children's pool, lockers, spa and steam rooms in addition to an expanded weight training center, aerobics and fitness studios, an elite 40-foot-high indoor bouldering and climbing wall all add to the enormous variety of athletics training options employees could participate in during their workday on campus.

Both the Bo Jackson Fitness Center and the Nike Sports Performance Center represent Nike's corporate commitment and belief in creating a workplace environment that immerses its employees in the world and culture of sports. The two-story, 75,000-square-foot facility sits on axis at the southern end of two international-sized soccer fields named after soccer great Cristiano Ronaldo. Three sand volleyball courts in addition to four outdoor basketball courts anchor the southern end of the site linking directly to a 2.5-mile running trail that weaves throughout the campus. During the design of the center, Nike elected to add to the program a new 400-meter (1,312-foot) outdoor running track that we imbedded directly into a dense forest of trees, creating a unique one-of-a-kind experience for runners passing through tall stands of trees and open meadows.

Exterior materials reflect the language of the campus buildings and are clad in white composite aluminum panels expressing the building's form and strong graphic features, while the interior materials have been kept to a minimum using black slate floors and accents of eastern white maple.

The building is the second major fitness center on the campus, and aimed to expand on the provision of new sports facilities, including an 11-lane, 25-meter (82-foot) swimming pool.

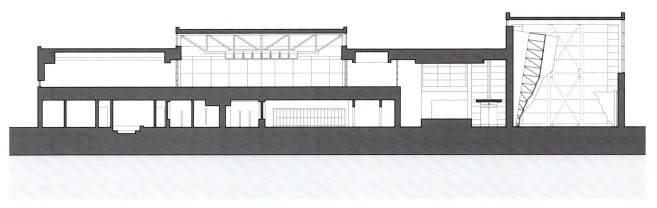

SECTION

NIKE SPORTS PERFORMANCE CENTER

Exterior materials reflect the language of the campus buildings. The white composite aluminum panels express the building's form and strong graphic features.

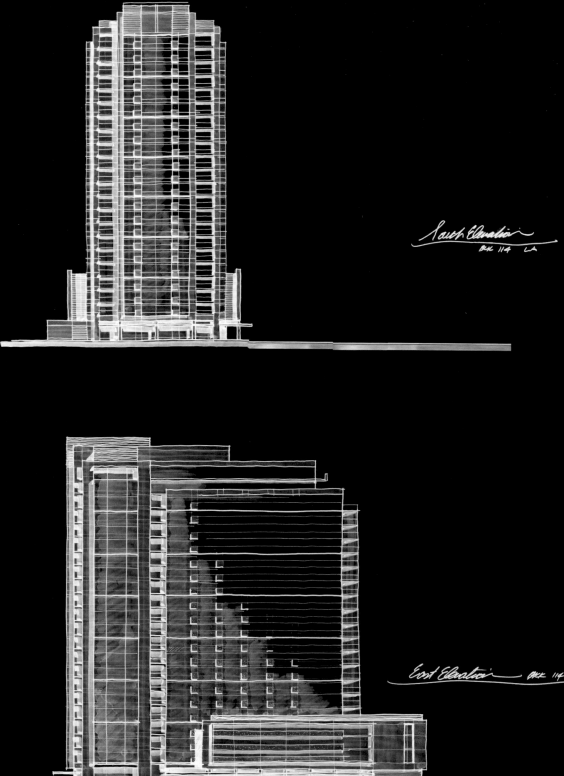

RESIDENTIAL, HOUSING & HOSPITALITY

ALDEN/DRUMMOND RESIDENCE

PORTLAND, OREGON | 1989 | 3,800 SQ FT

The Alden/Drummond Residence, designed for a professional couple with an extensive art collection, is situated on the edge of a steep hillside one mile from the heart of downtown Portland. The residence's relationship with the local context and its position along the west-facing slope of the hill are the key drivers that defined the design of the house. The 3,800-square-foot three-story home is bound on the north and west by the Hoyt Arboretum, a major inner-city public park. Volumetrically the house presents a very opaque sculpted façade that addresses the public street. A screened lap pool contained by solid six-foot stucco walls is situated in the front yard of the home, obscuring views into the living spaces yet allowing privacy from those rooms to views that spill out over the pool to the east and into the park to the west. The garage and guest bedrooms form the lowest level of the home and act as a podium or plinth that elevates the living spaces up to the street level. The living level is an open plan consisting of the entry, living, dining, and kitchen spaces that flow out onto private gardens and the pool terrace, enabling people to engage with the site and the adjacent park. The top floor is occupied by a private master suite and an open study with views over the living spaces and pool below.

The geometric composition and form of the house speak to solids and voids that ensure privacy from the public street and provide expansive open views to the surrounding park to the west. The design allows the surrounding landscape and public park to animate the living spaces of the house with the changing weather and natural light.

The living level is an open plan, consisting of the entry, living, and dining spaces that flow out onto private gardens and the pool terrace.

ALDEN/DRUMMOND RESIDENCE

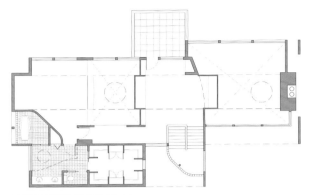

UPPER LEVEL FLOOR PLAN

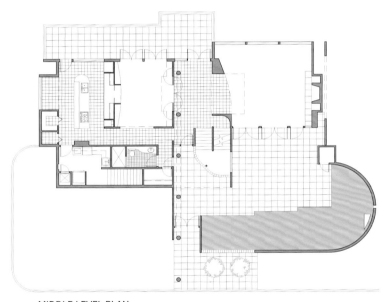

MIDDLE LEVEL PLAN

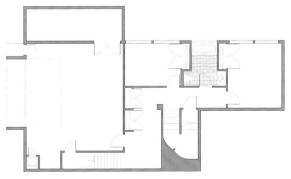

LOWER LEVEL FLOOR PLAN

The upper floor contains the private master quarters consisting of an open study with views over the living space below as well as the master bedroom that looks out over the Hoyt Arboretum.

ALDEN/DRUMMOND RESIDENCE

The plan is set up on a north–south axis providing layered views through the entire length of the house.

CRABBE RESIDENCE

PORTLAND, OREGON | 2000 | 5,100 SQ FT

Situated on a steeply sloping site in the West Hills of Portland, this single-family residence commands a 280-degree sweeping view of the city as well as the Cascade mountain range beyond. The two-story house contains two bedrooms, living, dining, kitchen, study, exercise rooms, as well as a large wine room, and a 60-foot lap pool. The shape of the floor plan is in direct response to capturing the view beyond. Exterior materials consist of exposed poured-in-place concrete walls, and stucco with stainless-steel railings and granite cobble at the entry drive. Like the exterior, interior finishes have been kept to a minimum consisting of smooth drywall, maple hardwood floors, and stainless-steel railings.

CRABBE RESIDENCE

Exterior materials consist of exposed poured-in-place concrete walls, and stucco with stainless-steel railings and granite cobble at the entry drive.

CRABBE RESIDENCE

The two-story residence with a 60-foot lap pool offers commanding views over the city and the Cascade mountain range.

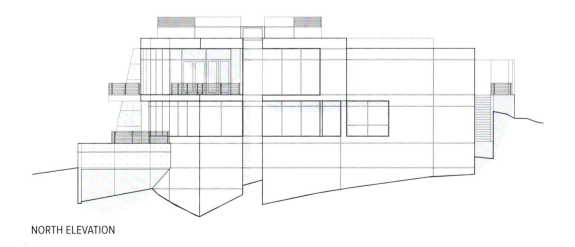

NORTH ELEVATION

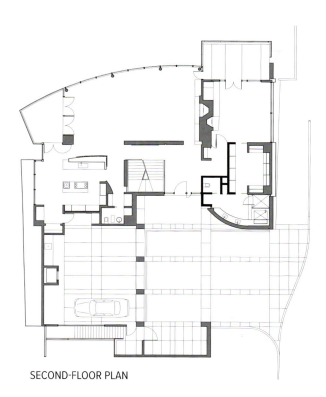

SECOND-FLOOR PLAN

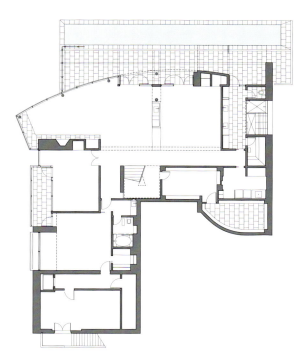

FIRST-FLOOR PLAN

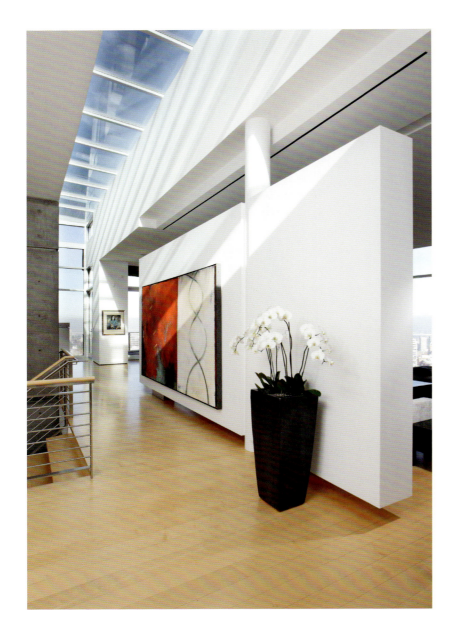

Interior finishes have been kept to a minimum consisting of smooth drywall, maple hardwood floors, and stainless-steel railings.

FRANKEL RESIDENCE

SISTERS, OREGON | 2006 | 3,200 SQ FT

The Frankel Residence is a single-family home composed of three distinct pavilions that allow the residence to be partitioned into different sizes when in use. Clad in stucco, these elements are connected together with wood-clad and glazed passageways that open to the landscaped spine and views beyond. The composition is constructed of a concrete plinth that raises the residence and outdoor living areas above the arid natural landscape, and provides areas for maintained landscape plantings. A concrete wall at the entry helps form a semi-enclosed courtyard. Extending the overall length of the composition is a horizontal landscape element planted in lawn and punctuated with a double allée of Swedish aspen trees.

The residence replaced a trailer that served as temporary housing on the site for years. The open-plan main pavilion has soaring 14-foot-high ceilings and contains the great room consisting of living space, dining room and kitchen, a master bedroom suite, offices and a powder room. The second pavilion houses a guest suite consisting of two bedrooms, sitting room, and bathroom; and is accessed by a short stair run. Both of these pavilions open to the landscape for outdoor living. An art studio that can accommodate overflow guests with a fold-out bed, laundry area, and two-car garage with storage are located in the third pavilion.

Central Oregon has great temperature swings throughout the year. Twelve-foot-deep overhangs on the west elevation face the main western view and shield the fully glazed main living space from the intense summer sun and heavy winter snow. This gesture creates exterior rooms that are open to the views and further protected from the sun by horizontal grillwork. Full-height glazing on the east elevation allows the residence to receive solar gain in the mornings and view the agricultural activities to the east. In addition to window and door fenestrations to the views, the main pavilion is open internally in the north–south direction with protected clerestory glass at each end.

The living room and master bedroom each orient themselves to a fireplace with a raised sitting hearth whose chimneys protrude as major design elements expressed on the exterior of the house. The main living pavilion is transparent on both the east and west elevations allowing dramatic views to the coast range to the west and a private courtyard to the east. Interior finishes are mahogany floors and casework, painted drywall, and some stone.

No trees were removed during construction and the natural ground cover has been encouraged to return back to the concrete plinth rising from the ground. This project includes future plans for a horse barn and arena to replace the existing stables. The remainder of the property is still farmed for alfalfa.

FRANKEL RESIDENCE

The single-family residence is broken into three distinct pavilions tied together with connecting glazed walkways bisected by a linear grove of Swedish aspen trees.

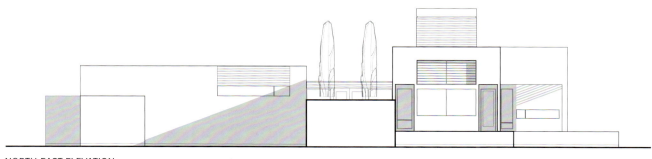

NORTH-EAST ELEVATION

FRANKEL RESIDENCE

No trees were removed during construction and the natural ground cover has been encouraged to return back to the concrete plinth rising from the ground. Interior finishes are mahogany floors and casework, painted drywall, and some stone.

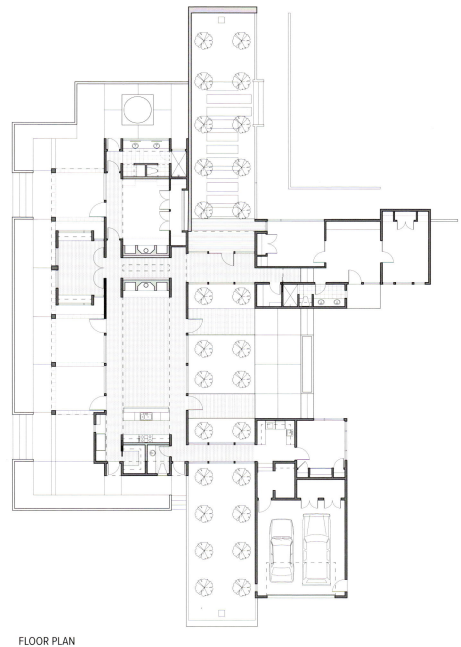

FLOOR PLAN

The open-plan main pavilion has soaring 14-foot-high ceilings and contains the great room consisting of living space, dining room, and kitchen.

FRITZ RESIDENCE

LAKE OSWEGO, OREGON | 2020 | 6,100 SQ FT

Located eight miles south of Portland on Lake Oswego, this private residence for a family of five was designed as a sanctuary and a retreat for its owners who were seeking privacy and space for reflection and contemplation. The lake surrounds the site on three sides affording all interior spaces unparalleled views of the water and surrounding hills. The residence is notable not only for the expansive views of the lake but also the richness of the experience as one approaches the house from the public street to the front door. The design concept speaks to the relationship of openness and compression as one approaches the house passing through moments of containment at the entry courtyards to wide-open distance views across the lake through dramatic two-story glazed volumes as one enters the home.

The structure, form, and orientation of the house are all a direct response to the makeup of the site. Defined by two long rectangular wings that come together at the main entry, one arrives through an intimate courtyard comprising reflecting ponds and the sound of water. As one enters the house the wings part and open out toward the lake framing a two-story volume with the living room forming the heart of the plan. Interior rooms are organized to create multiple outdoor courtyards and private sitting areas for privacy and introspection. All living and dining spaces are located on the main level with a direct connection to the lake and the outdoors, while the second level contains the private quarters of the home with bedrooms suites and a meditation studio.

The exterior skin of the building is clad in a smooth stucco painted in a soft deep dusky gray color while all exterior window shrouds and horizontal sunscreens are finished in a deep gunmetal gray, softening the volume of the building mass while adding rich detail and shadow.

The residence is notable not only for the expansive views of the lake but also the richness of the experience as one approaches the house from the public street to the front door.

As one enters the house the wings part and open out toward the lake.

FRITZ RESIDENCE

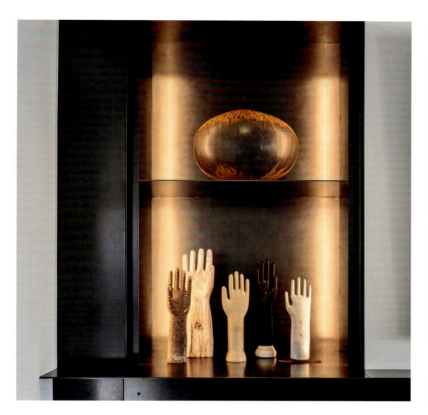

FRITZ RESIDENCE

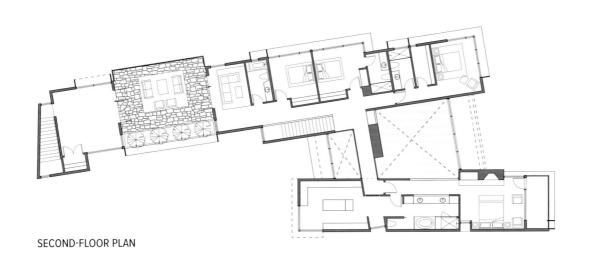

The floor plan consists of two distinct "bars" that fan open toward the lake framing the living room that forms the heart of the home. Raised landscape planters reinforce the geometry of the house plan providing privacy while framing dramatic views to the lake beyond.

SECOND-FLOOR PLAN

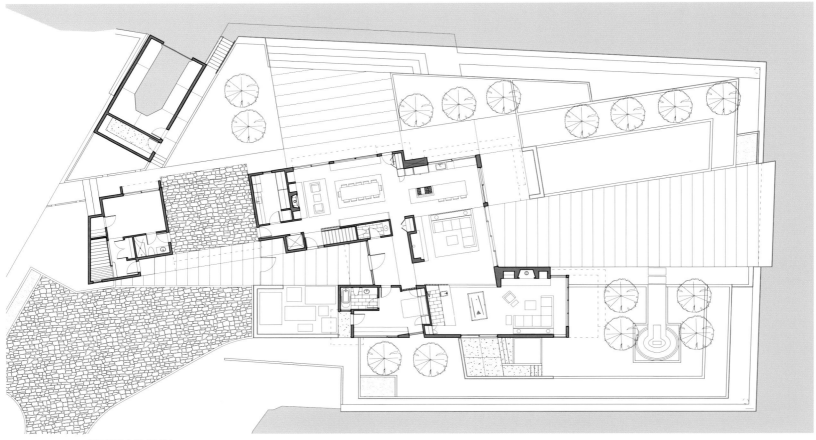

FIRST-FLOOR PLAN

FRITZ RESIDENCE

The addition of multiple outdoor courtyards and private sitting areas allow private space for introspection.

WEST HILLS RESIDENCE

PORTLAND, OREGON | 2005 | 3,800 SQ FT

The 3,800-square-foot three-story single-family residence occupies a prominent location at the end of a quarter-mile drive at the top of a half-acre site one mile west of downtown Portland. Perched on a level plateau, the site offers major views to the Oregon Coast mountain range to the west as well as over the suburban community of Beaverton below. The linear floor plan aligned along a north–south axis is essentially one room deep in an effort to maximize views through the house to the distant views to the west as well as opening onto more intimate and contained courtyard views nestled into a large grove of trees to the east.

The program called for the residence to be defined by three distinct zones where the lowest level would contain the guest suite, a family room, and a third bedroom. Coupled with the garage as well as an outdoor pool, this level creates the base or podium for the building. The second floor is accessed by way of an external staircase located along an east–west axis that bisects the plan that takes guests from the auto court up to the main living level of the house. The third floor or main level is dedicated to family living and entertaining. Living, dining, and family rooms as well as a kitchen and a study all open out onto private ground-level courtyards. Level three occupies the top floor of the building and is zoned as private for sleeping containing the master suite as well as a secondary bedroom.

Perforated stainless-steel mesh panels form a translucent sunscreen over the west facing two-story window wall to significantly reduce the solar gain on the interior living space. Oversized glazed windows allow for views to the lap pool, a separate guesthouse, and the extensive outdoor gardens that are nestled in a park-like setting.

Perforated stainless-steel mesh panels form a translucent sunscreen over the west facing two-story window wall to significantly reduce the solar gain on the interior living space. The internal staircase and flooring showcase the beauty of natural wood.

WEST HILLS RESIDENCE

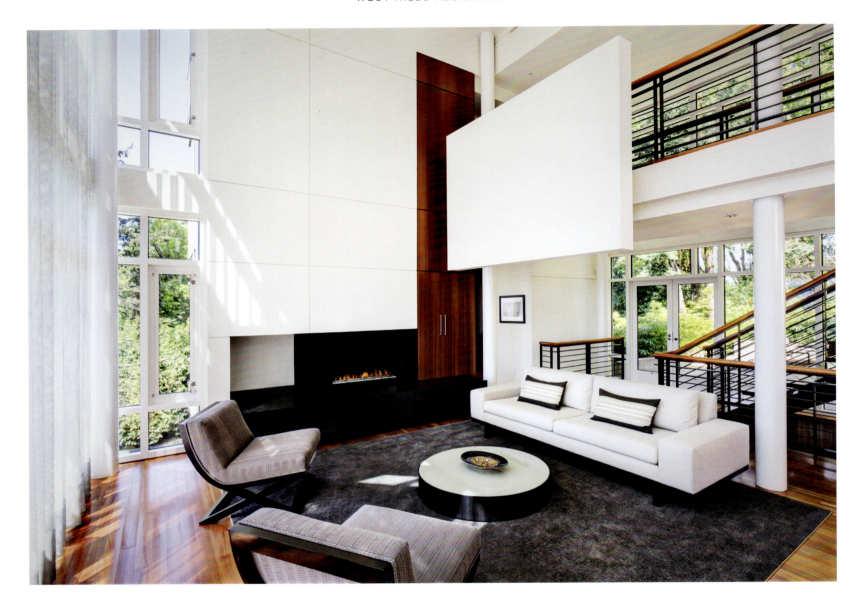

Oversized glazed windows allow for views to the lap pool, a separate guesthouse, and the extensive outdoor gardens that are nestled in a park-like setting.

WEST HILLS RESIDENCE

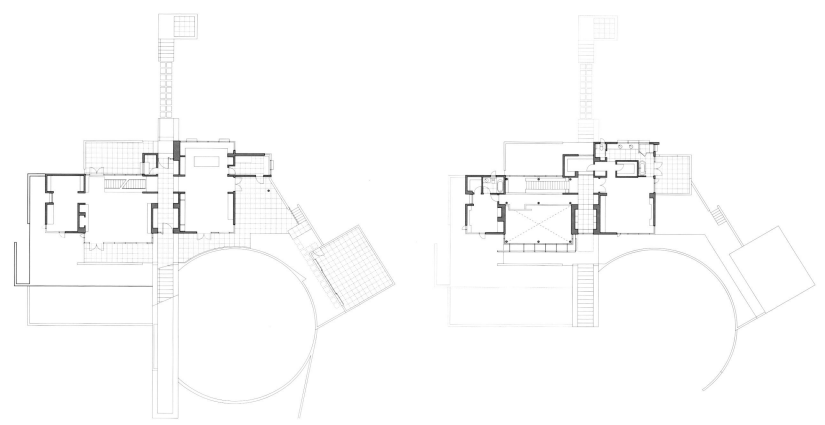

SECOND-FLOOR PLAN

THIRD-FLOOR PLAN

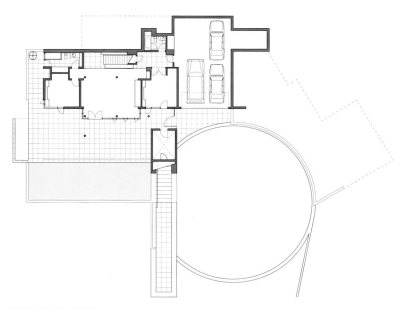

FIRST-FLOOR PLAN

PEARL APARTMENTS

PORTLAND, OREGON | EXPECTED COMPLETION 2022 | 39,000 SQ FT

Through simple architectural forms and materials, the design for this apartment block is a modern adaptation of the city's historic warehouse language. Located in an area where historically shipping and receiving operations occurred, it was common for most structures in this district to provide elevated docks on the first floor. This architectural feature informed the design of Pearl Apartment's base. The continuation of an elevated pedestrian sidewalk on the east façade naturally follows from the adjacent property under an industrial canopy, stepping down to the street elevation at the building corner.

The seven-story 66-unit apartment building is clad in a dark gunmetal-colored brick with accents of black industrial ribbed metals and light-colored wooden windows to create a simple elegant mix of materials that references the historic palette of many of the historic buildings in the district. Oversized 10-foot-high wood-framed operable windows and doors differentiate the lower base of the building from the upper floors, articulated by punched openings in the masonry block. The regular pattern of the windows on the residential floors reflects the column and beam spacing of the building's structure. Private balconies along the south and east elevation are articulated by deep metal shrouds that frame the grouping of windows into playful geometric patterns adding shadow and depth to the building elevations.

Driven by a desire to provide highly compact Japanese-style micro-units, the developers of Pearl Apartments worked with TVA to provide units composed of studios ranging from 300 square feet to two-bedroom units at 688 square feet.

The Pearl District located in Portland's downtown urban core was a major industrial district as recently as 1985 consisting primarily of one- to four-story industrial buildings that were served by freight trains and trucking. With the explosive growth in Portland's population during the 1990s, the district became the center of a major revitalization with the development of mid-rise high-density housing and first-floor retail that that has grown into one of Portland's most expensive districts for high-end living.

THE PEARL APARTMENTS

JOHN ROSS TOWER

PORTLAND, OREGON | 2007 | 576,800 SQ FT | LEED GOLD

The John Ross Tower is one of the most distinct high-rise projects in Portland's renowned South Waterfront development and one of the first signature buildings in the district's "architects series"—a visionary approach to diversifying the look and feel of the neighborhood, and to distinguish it from such areas as the Pearl District. As one of six architects to be selected to design a new tower in the district, the collaboration with my fellow peers was rewarding and inspiring as we worked together to create a new live-work community for Portland.

Boasting a slender, uniquely elliptical design, the John Ross Tower embodies Portland's exceptional style of high-density living, offering breathtaking vistas, and close proximity to all the amenities and cultural offerings of a dynamic urban center.

At 31 stories and rising 325 feet from ground level, the tower is currently the tallest residential building in Oregon. Encompassing 470,000 square feet above-grade, it features 303 condominium residences, townhouses, first-floor retail, and underground parking. An L-shaped podium embraces the tower and creates a garden courtyard, while the apex is capped by a stunning 5,000-square-foot penthouse with 360-degree views. Dramatic vistas expand in all directions—east to the snow-covered slopes of Mt. Hood, west to Portland's distinctive West Hills, north to the city's burgeoning downtown with neighboring Mt. St. Helens in the distance, and south to the Willamette River and beyond. Twenty-foot floor-to-floor heights on the lower retail level provide tremendous transparency, while an adjoining quarter-block park, activated by retail, offers a seating area for an outdoor café, and allows visitors to move diagonally through the block. The tower provides an engaging pedestrian scale at street level, while its unusual, slender, elliptical form preserves dramatic view corridors in the densely populated neighborhood, and channels sunlight to ground level.

The high-rise tower is a slender elliptical design that helps preserve views of homes located in the adjacent West Hills. Landing on a four-story podium that reinforces the block edges, additional height was granted by the city in exchange for the creation of a quarter-block pocket park shared by the three adjacent condominium towers.

JOHN ROSS TOWER

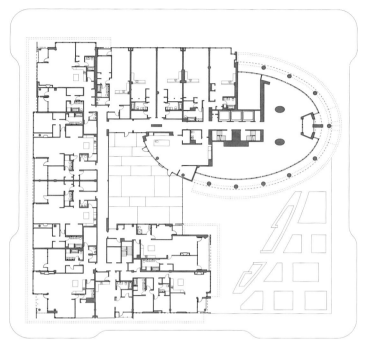

SECOND-FLOOR PLAN

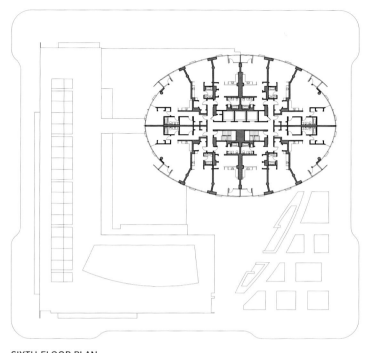

SIXTH-FLOOR PLAN

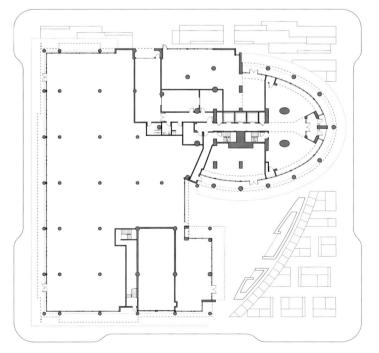

FIRST-FLOOR PLAN

JOHN ROSS TOWER

The tower, the first of the signature buildings in the district, is currently the tallest residential building in Oregon. An L-shaped podium embraces the tower and creates a garden courtyard.

GOOSE HOLLOW LOFTS

PORTLAND, OREGON | 2018 | 58,000 SQ FT

Located in the heart of Portland's downtown Goose Hollow Neighborhood, the Goose Hollow Lofts is a five-story 66-unit market-rate apartment project located adjacent to Portland State University. The project was designed to support the student population that occupies the majority of the rental market in the district. The individual apartments, averaging 480 square feet in area, consist primarily of studio and one-bedroom living units that are highly efficient and offer students alternative living options to residing on campus. The design approach was to maximize the allowable buildable area of the site while keeping the form and massing of the building simple and compact. Clad in ribbed-metal siding and board-formed concrete, the lofts speak to an industrial language that reflects many of the existing buildings that make up the character of the neighborhood. Windows are articulated with extruded metal shrouds that act as partial sunscreens as well as architectural elements that reinforce the geometry and playful patterning of the exterior façade. At a total of 58,000 square feet, all units in the complex are positioned to take maximum advantage of city views to the east and the West Hills to the south. The building maintains the urban street wall to the north along SW Jefferson St with high bay live-work units occupying the first floor opening to small outdoor terraces in an effort to activate and energize the evolving neighborhood.

Portland has been experiencing explosive growth throughout its collective neighborhoods that make up its urban core. Much of that growth is reflected in the development of new multistory apartment buildings responding to the influx of a rapid growing population in support of new and expanding companies that are calling Portland home.

Located in the downtown core next to Portland State University, the apartment block was designed to accommodate student living. Unit sizes consist of small one-bedroom and studio apartments that take full advantage of the spectacular views over the city skyline.

All units in the complex are positioned to take maximum advantage of city views to the east and the West Hills to the south. Windows are articulated with extruded metal shrouds that act as partial sunscreens.

GOOSE HOLLOW LOFTS

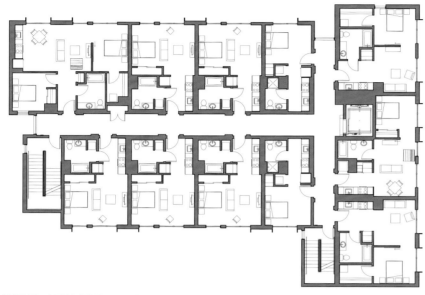

SECOND–SIXTH TYPICAL FLOOR PLAN

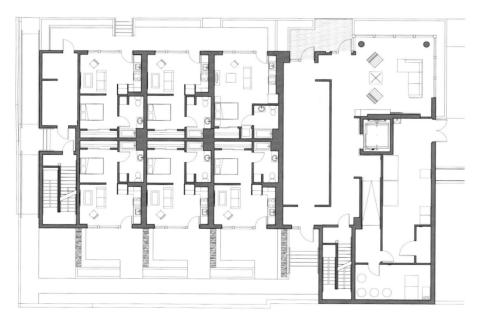

FIRST-FLOOR PLAN

The colorful lobby offers a bright welcome for visitors.

EVO TOWER

LOS ANGELES, CALIFORNIA | 2008 | 503,200 SQ FT | LEED SILVER

Located in the heart of the vibrant Los Angeles's live entertainment district, this LEED Silver condominium tower embodies high-density urban living while incorporating sustainable materials, environmentally responsible construction techniques, and a thoughtful approach to neighborhood growth and planning.

The 24-story tower encompasses 500,000 square feet above-grade, 311 high-end condominium units, and five two-story, street-level townhomes. A three-level underground parking garage accommodates 425 vehicles.

The top-floor lounge features luxurious seating and expansive views showcasing the city skyline and beyond. An outdoor fireplace and lounge seating area creates an inviting gathering place adjacent to the building's fitness center. The experience is complemented by the expansive Sixth Floor Terrace, featuring an open-air pool and spa, an outdoor kitchen, lounge-seating, and lush greenscaping.

Thompson's design of the building and site promotes a holistic approach to sustainable green living and quality of life. Unique architectural features include an exterior envelope curtain wall system with high-efficiency glazing, recycled aluminum window mullions, and metal panels. The design unites large elevations of clear glazing with carefully composed lines of metallic paneling, utilizing reflection and sheen to change moods with the day, reflecting sky in daylight and turning transparent at night.

The street landscape design enhances the urban environment and encourages and supports pedestrian activity to further reinforce the vitality and the unique characteristics of the neighborhood. A ground-level courtyard provides a park-like setting open to the public. Landscaped infiltration planters mitigate water pollution by reducing impervious areas, remove contaminants from stormwater runoff, and provide additional softscape.

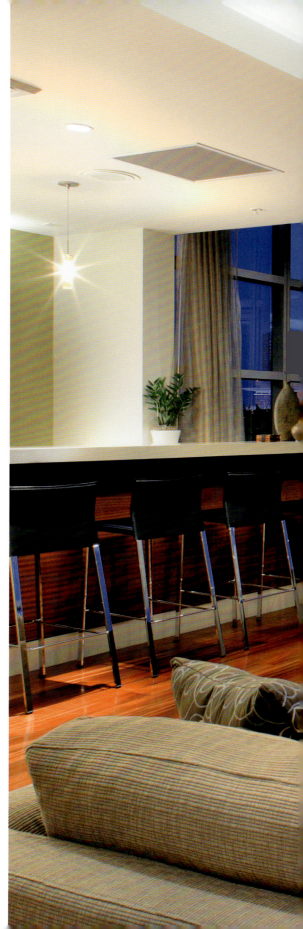

EVO TOWER

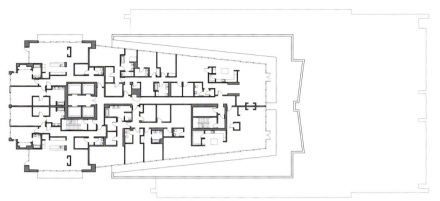

23RD-FLOOR PLAN

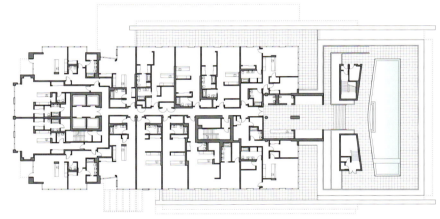

SIXTH-FLOOR PLAN

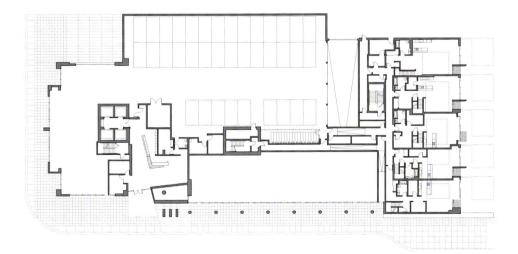

FIRST-FLOOR PLAN

THE ANIVA APARTMENTS

PORTLAND, OREGON | 2019 | 46,800 SQ FT

An innovative transit-oriented development, the Aniva Apartments project is a 90-unit, five-story multifamily apartment building located in the Overlook neighborhood of Portland. The Aniva Apartments provide market-rate housing with a mixture of studio and one-bedroom dwellings. The project is a symbol of ongoing community investments that are occurring along MLK Boulevard on one of Portland's busy light-rail lines with direct access to the inner city core.

The building façade is broken up into distinct volumes articulated with varying materials and setbacks that make the building compatible with the smaller scaled structures that define the district. Fronting the light-rail line, the base of the building is composed of live-work units with direct access to the street, creating an environment that is inviting to pedestrians and transit users. Upper floors share dramatic views over the Portland skyline and the Cascade mountain range to the east. The building is clad in ribbed and smooth composite metal panels forming a simple elegant envelope that is articulated with extruded metal shrouds that group windows into playful geometric patterns, adding drama and depth to the building elevations.

The Overlook district consists of evolving neighborhoods all in transition due to its location only one mile from the city core. Fifteen years ago the city extended its light-rail line down MLK Boulevard, which has acted as a major catalyst for development of new multilevel apartment buildings, bringing new life, energy, and vitality to these older neighborhoods. Street-level restaurants, new stores, and businesses have emerged along the streetcar line, inspiring a surge in both new and renovated homes.

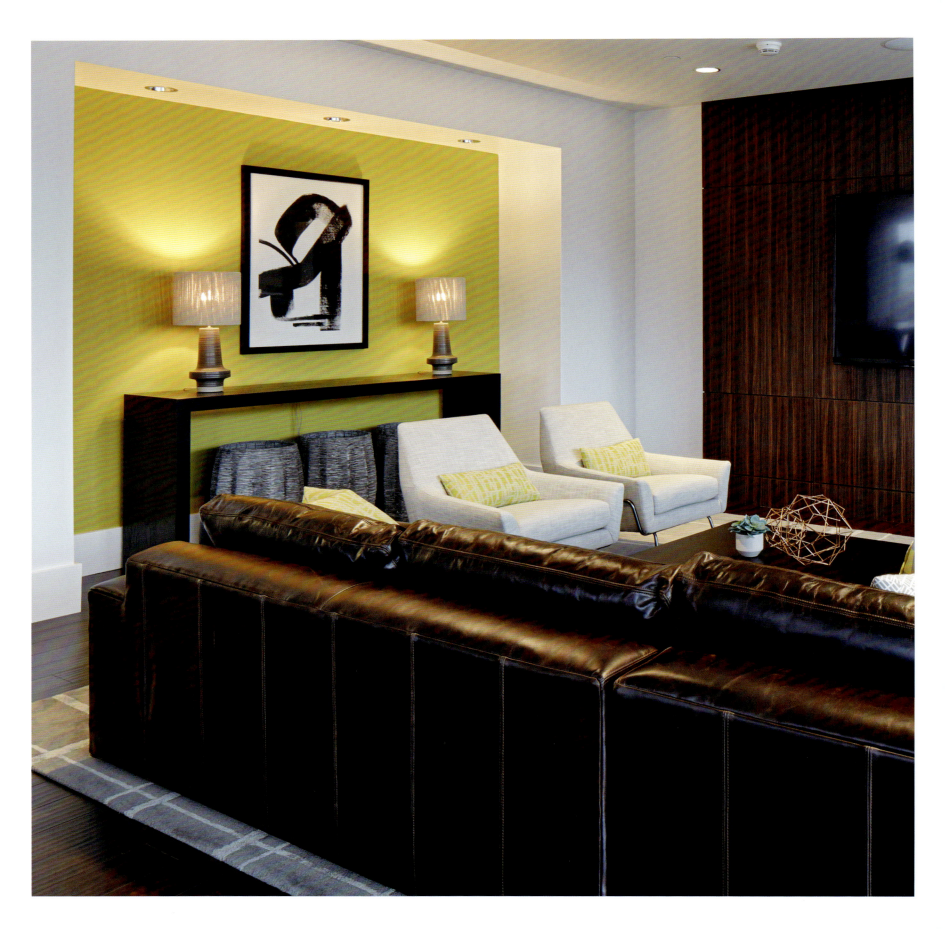

THE ANIVA APARTMENTS

The communal lobby offers a warm and inviting space for residents.

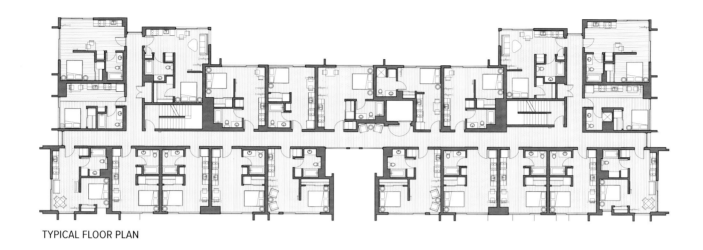

TYPICAL FLOOR PLAN

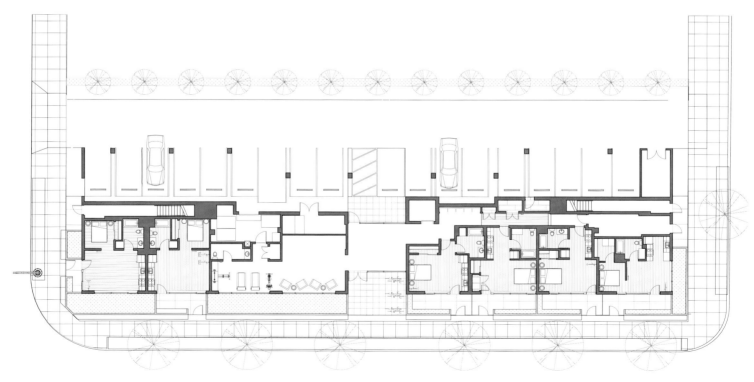

FIRST-FLOOR PLAN

THE CARING CABIN

PACIFIC CITY, OREGON | 2004 | 4,110 SQ FT

Inspired by the memory of Alexandra Ellis, a courageous five-year-old with a gift for bringing people together, the Caring Cabin is the result of numerous individuals, businesses, and organizations donating their talents, time, and vision to create an extraordinary place for healing and renewal of the human spirit. The Children's Cancer Association sought to provide a lakeside retreat in the mountains at the Oregon coast where families of critically ill children could escape the sterile environments of the medical world, and enjoy time with family and the serenity of nature to create their own lasting memories. Nestled among donated land comprising 24 wooded acres in Pacific City on the Oregon coast, the Caring Cabin provides that opportunity. Over $1.2 million in monies, materials, and energy were donated to this project—the first of its kind in the western region of the United States.

Designed as a series of interconnected pavilions, the retreat is defined by the main residence, a small meditation pavilion, and a recreation room with a sleeping loft over a two-car garage. The main facility comprises two private family bedroom pavilions or suites and an adjacent family gathering pavilion including kitchen, dining, and informal gathering spaces, focused on a large monolithic basalt fireplace that defines the heart of the house. The vaulted pavilions are each linked by a connecting circulation spine defined by a lower flat roof creating a dynamic play of interconnecting shed forms that express the plan three-dimensionally. Wrapped with glass walls, the corners of the pavilions allow connection with the outdoors via views of the lake and surrounding forest and flood the exposed wood-framed interior spaces with the warmth of natural light. The building pavilions are structured using exposed glue-laminated timbers and wood decking along with native basalt stone used on fireplaces and the exterior site wall that all speak to indigenous materials found at the site and along the Oregon coastline.

THE CARING CABIN

Designed as a series of interconnected pavilions, the retreat is defined by the main residence, a small meditation pavilion, and a recreation room with a sleeping loft over a two-car garage.

THE CARING CABIN

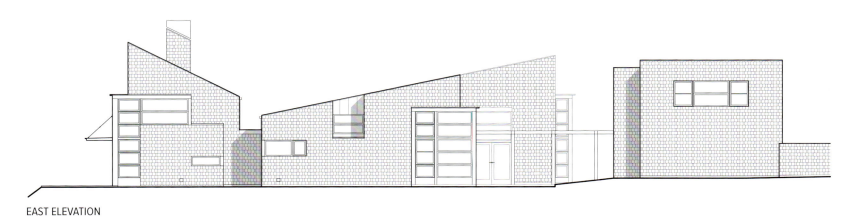

EAST ELEVATION

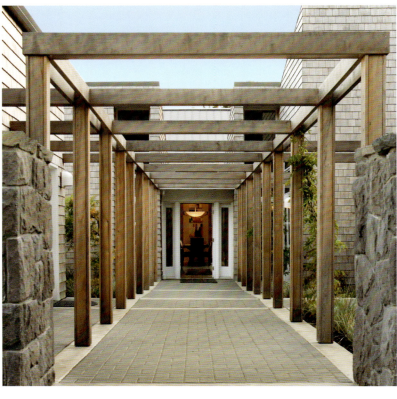

THE CARING CABIN

A large open living/dining room and kitchen form the great room of the retreat where family members gather to share time while taking in expansive views out to the natural coastal landscape that envelopes the site.

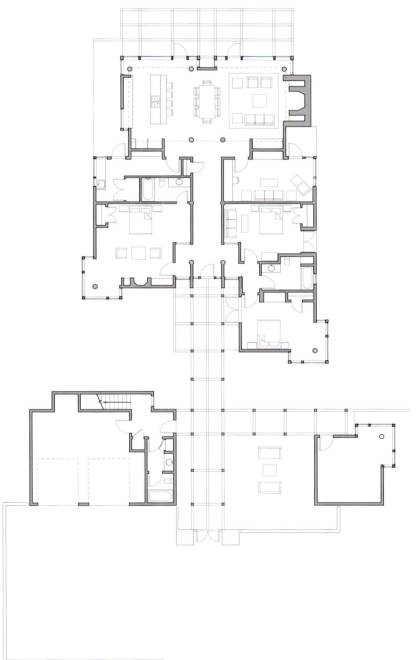

FLOOR PLAN

GREVE RESIDENCE

PORTLAND, OREGON | 2019 | 5,100 SQ FT

The site for this private residence located in the West Hills of Portland is populated with dense mature trees that afford both privacy and seclusion from adjacent homes in a neighborhood built in the early 1950s. Designed for a growing family of four and their extended family, the courtyard scheme allows for natural light to pass through all public areas of the house throughout the day while forming a central heart or focus to the plans with private internal views shared by surrounding rooms.

All rooms open out to private exterior courtyards that engage the dense surrounding natural landscape, offering outdoor gardens for areas of contemplation and private reflection as well as family gatherings. The home is clad in white stucco with poured-in-place board-formed concrete courtyard walls that anchor the home to the landscape while adding privacy and a layered dimension to the building geometry. The building plan consists of two horizontal living bars connected with a 14-foot-high glazed living/dining room aligned to allow layered views through the central courtyard to a landscaped garden and outdoor living space beyond. Exterior horizontal sunscreens allow filtered managed light to penetrate deep into the living space minimizing solar heat gain from the early morning and late afternoon sun.

The interior finish palette is minimal, consisting of riff-cut white-oak floors and cabinetry accented with blackened steel panels. The connection of indoor to outdoor space is seamless and reinforced throughout the house by the incorporation of large sliding doors and windows.

Private courtyards engage the dense surrounding natural landscape, offering views through the house to the outdoor gardens beyond.

GREVE RESIDENCE

SECOND-FLOOR PLAN

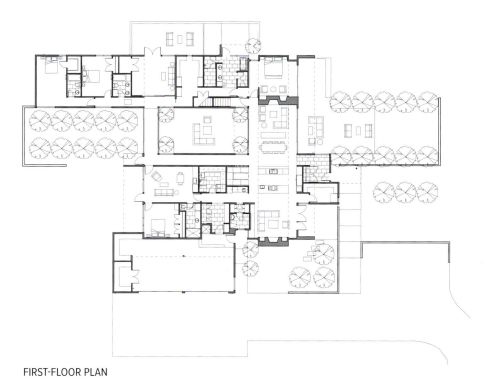

FIRST-FLOOR PLAN

The courtyard scheme allows natural light to pass through the house while forming a central heart with private internal views shared by surrounding rooms.

VANCOUVER WATERFRONT CONDOMINIUM TOWER

VANCOUVER, WASHINGTON | EXPECTED COMPLETION 2024 | 167,000 SQ FT

Located along the banks of the Columbia River, the Vancouver Waterfront Condominium Tower is designed to become a new urban landmark in the city of Vancouver, Washington. Often viewed as a bedroom community of Portland, development of this new mixed-use district is redefining the city, bringing new office buildings and residential housing along with restaurants and retail to its downtown core. The design of the tower is an expression of modern architecture providing unique high-quality housing with unparalleled views of downtown Portland, the Columbia River, and the Cascade mountain range beyond. The building is composed of two distinct towers of differing heights connected by a common core. Each unit takes maximum advantage of river views and averages only six units per floor.

The 66-unit, 167,000-square-foot condominium tower stands 13 stories high, and is clad in white composite aluminum panels. The formal, ordered geometric façades are highly articulated with balconies, stepped façades, and sunscreens that create dramatic shadows and depth when viewed from afar in both daytime and at night. The massing of the tower is simple and elegant and is stitched together with interlocking planes composed of a light-colored skin that play off its composition of solids and voids. The fundamental drivers that shaped the tower design are specific to maximizing the views from all units, the quality of light entering the plan throughout the day as well as its relationship to the river and the context of the city.

VANCOUVER WATERFRONT CONDOMINIUM TOWER

SECOND-FLOOR PLAN

12TH-FLOOR PLAN

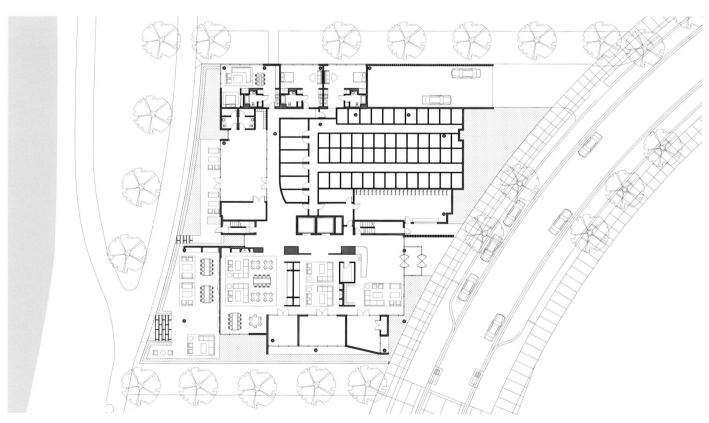

FIRST-FLOOR PLAN

ALDER 9 APARTMENTS

PORTLAND, OREGON | EXPECTED COMPLETION 2024 | 130,000 SQ FT

Alder 9 is a nine-story, 173-unit urban infill apartment project located in the inner southeast industrial section of downtown Portland, Oregon. The new market-rate apartments will celebrate Portland's tradition of mixed-use high-density urban infill housing focused on revitalizing older industrial neighborhoods throughout the city. With a unit mix of predominantly studio and one-bedroom units, living units average 350 to 500 square feet per unit and are competitively priced, focusing on attracting a younger cross section of renters in an effort to continue the densification of Portland's inner city. The U-shaped plan maximizes views from all units to the skyline of downtown Portland as well as the Cascade mountain range to the east. Located blocks from Portland's streetcar line, the project is served by the city's extensive mass transportation system reducing the direct need for cars.

The building skin is composed of a highly expressive geometric grid pattern clad in composite white metal panels that are reminiscent of the exposed structural grids of load-bearing exterior walls that were commonplace in the historic construction of industrial buildings that make up the architecture of the neighborhood. The grids are infilled with brick and ribbed-metal panels that form the window bays of the building with industrial materials used in a contemporary manner.

The building will occupy a 100-by-200-foot site with the street level containing retail lease space as well as apartment amenities that will activate the pedestrian experience as well as provide commercial restaurants and businesses needed to support the evolving neighborhood. On level two, a large light-filled courtyard will become the outdoor living room and amenity area for the tenants while the roof on level nine will provide highly desired entertainment areas sharing expansive views over the city and the surrounding neighborhood.

ALDER 9 APARTMENTS

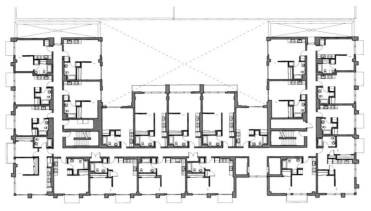

TYPICAL FLOOR PLAN

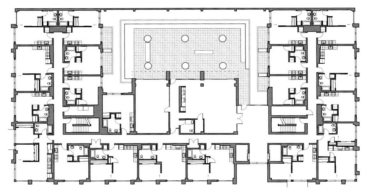

SECOND-FLOOR PLAN

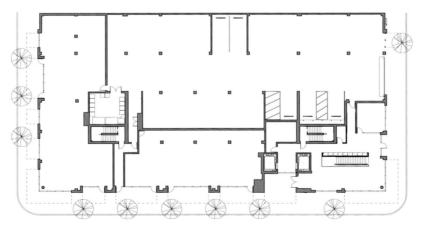

FIRST-FLOOR PLAN

The building skin is composed of a highly expressive geometric grid pattern reminiscent of the exposed structural grids of load-bearing exterior walls that were commonplace in the industrial buildings that make up the architecture of the neighborhood.

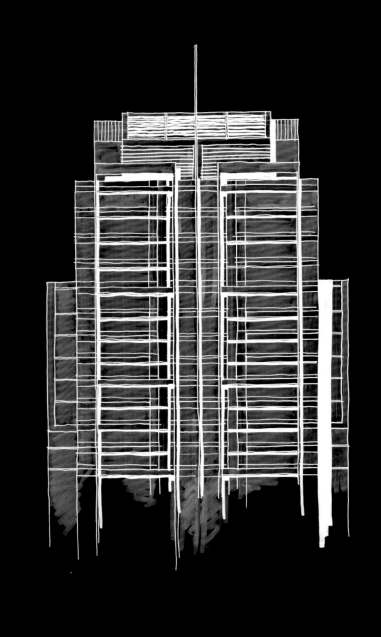

APPENDIX

BIOGRAPHY

As founder and Design Principal of Portland-based TVA Architects, Robert Thompson received his architectural training at the University of Oregon, graduating in 1977 with honors. He went on to intern in the office of Skidmore, Owings & Merrill where he was heavily influenced by the firm's commitment to early modernism and the International Style of contemporary architecture. He established TVA Architects in 1984 and has grown the firm to include four principals and a staff of 40 collaborators. His work has included major commissions throughout the United States and Asia with work focused on the design and branding of major corporate campuses for Fortune 500 clients, including Nike, Inc., Procter & Gamble, Sony Ericsson, Chico's, and Banfield Pet Hospital, as well as museums, institutional buildings, sports facilities, high-rise office and residential towers, and single-family residences. TVA has received over 54 local, national, and international awards for excellence in design, including 37 from the American Institute of Architects.

In 1993 Thompson was the youngest American architect to be inducted into the AIA College of Fellows, the institute's highest honor, for his contribution to the profession of architecture in the category of design. The firm's body of work has been published internationally in leading journals, including *Architecture*, *Architectural Record*, *Progressive Architecture*, *Metropolis*, and *Fortune Magazine*. In 2000 Italian publisher L'Arca Edizioni published a monograph detailing the firm's early work. Thompson has served on numerous AIA design award juries throughout the United States. In 1997 he was honored to be selected to jury the National AIA Honor Awards program in Washington, D.C.

In addition to his professional practice Robert has kept ties with the University of Oregon School of Architecture and Allied Arts serving on their Board of Visitors as well as teaching design studios and serving as guest critic over the years. He has been a guest lecturer on his work at universities and organizations, including Tongji University in Shanghai, China, SCI-ARC, University of Nebraska, University of Washington, Proctor & Gamble Headquarters, Washington State University, Rice University, the Portland Creative Conference, and UCLA School of Architecture and Urban Design.

Recent work includes the Park Avenue West Tower, a 30-story mixed-use high-rise in downtown Portland, the Matthew Knight Arena and Ford Alumni Center on the University of Oregon campus in Eugene, the new Vancouver corporate headquarters for Banfield Pet Hospital in Washington state, Nike, Inc.'s new 650,000-square-foot Asian campus located in Shanghai, China, a private aircraft hangar for Nike Chairman Phil Knight, the EVO and John Ross residential high-rise towers in Los Angeles and Portland, respectively, as well as 15 Nike retail stores across the United States. Thompson served as Nike, Inc.'s principal design architect for over 28 years, completing three major new campuses in the United States and China, 51 new buildings, retail stores, and over 3.7 million square feet of corporate interiors for the world's leading footwear and apparel giant. The Nike World Headquarters was honored as the International Corporate Campus of the Year in 2001.

TVA EMPLOYEES & COLLABORATORS

1984–2021

Aaron B. Cook
Aaron Hall
Aaron J. Vanderpool
Alan Gerencer
Alexander Khesin
Alexandre X. Asselineau
Alexis Vaivoda
Allan Norris
Allison Cummings
Allyson Pease
Amanda S. Butler
Amarjit Singh Tamber
Amy Fewkes
Anastasia Perrigo
Andre DeBar
Andrew Brorson
Andrew Feinberg
Andrzej Babiracki
Anita D. Alastra
Anna Labadie
Anthony Martinez
Arthur Asgian
Aung Barteaux
Benjamin D. Stakely
Blake Thompson
Bonnie P. Chiu-Wong
Bonnie S. Shields
Boyce Postma
Brandon Francom
Brian Higgins
Brian M. Grosklos
Brien Costello
Brooks Thompson
Bruce Kenny

Caleb Mitchell
Calvert Helms
Carolyn Murray
Chariti Montez
Charlena C. Kea
Charles Bahlman
Charlie H. Neville
Cheryl Piha
Christopher Bischof
Christopher White
Chuck Salvador
Clark Brockman
Clint E. Cook
Colin Hedrick
Constantin Luchian
Courtney Miller
Craig Caramelli
Craig Witte
Daniel B. Bradbury
Daniel L. Childs
Daniel Gates
Daniel Gero
Daniel McFarland
Darin Dougherty
Darren Schroeder
David Brown
David Fittipaldi
David P. Gellos
David E. Morris
David Shubin
David L. Wolff
Deborah France
Deborah Roe
Diana L. Simmons

Dimitri C. Englert
Edward J. Bruin
Ehsan Iran Nejad
Elijah Elder
Elisa M. Rocha
Elizabeth L. Collins
Elizabeth N. Delorme
Ellen Hynson
Ellen Morrison
Ellen Yarnell
Emily Englund-Stellflug
Emily A. HagenBurger
Erez Russo
Eric Gamer
Eric A. Li
Eric Pfau
Erik F. Dorsett
Erin L. Brouilette
Ethan M. Schwanz
Florence R. Woodbury
Francis Dardis
George Hara
Gordon Gillan
Gregory Miller
Gregory S. Mitchell
Harley R. Cowan
Iain F. MacKenzie
Ivan Ponce
J. Peter Foster
Jackson Dyal
James Bocci
James Henry
James Smith
James Yamada

Jane Waren
Janet Foz Jacobs
Janice Fisher
Jared Z. Mayzak
Jaynie Ellis
Jeffrey Bromwell
Jeffrey Law
Jennifer Brocks
Jennifer Lee
Jeremy Spurgin
Jeremy Webber
Jerry Waters
Jesse Figgins
Jessica T. Pearre
Jim Bocci
Jim Henry
Jiselle M. Crawford
Joann Hermance
Joel Cota
Johannes Zech
John P. Boyd
John A. Eidman
John J. Gonzales
John Heili
John T. Heinen
John M. Jamiel
John Medvec
John Thomas
Jonas Rake
Joseph K. Morgan
Joshua Powell
Julio Rocha
Justin Hurley
Kathryn A. Seifert

Kelly C. Cady
Kelly Roemhildt
Kelsey Lovett
Kenneth Paulsen
Kevin Gernhardt
Kim Ilosvay
Kirsten K. Perkins
Kristin K. Jackson
Kurt Schultz
Kylee Campbell
Laura Eddings
Laura M. Sinsel
Leslie Cliffe
Lewis Chui
Linda Rice
Lisa Ann Christie
Luke M. Janzen
Mandy Huesman
Marc A. Labadie
Marcy E. Pierce
Marie M. Malone
Mark Annen
Mark Raggett
Mark D. Williams
Mary Jane Symes
Matt Piccone
Matthew B. Postma
Matthew D. Riordan
Meaghan A. Morawski
Melissa Mitchell
Michael Feinstein
Michael Gregg
Michael A. Hahn
Michael Payne
Michelle M. Lum
Mira Boumatar
Montgomery J. Hill
Morgan Pintarich
Nathan Corser
Ned Vaivoda
Neil Cristal
Nicholas P. Hemmer
Nicholas J. Williams
Nick Wentz
Nicole Hipp
Nikolas Boscanin
Noel Snodgrass
Pamela E. Saftler
Param Bedi
Patrick R. Sullivan
Patrick Tiland
Patsi Burbach
Paul Darmofal
Paul Fiema
Paul G. Maziar
Paul Oseth
Paul Smith
Paul Thimm
Pearse D. O'Moore
Peter Alef
Peter G. Wilmarth
Peter Zaik
Phil Lewellyn
Philip Krueger
Randy Williams
Raymond Cheng
Rena J. Ackley
Renee Kludas
Richard W. Rapp
Robert M. Curry
Robert Hager
Robert Ilosvay
Robert A. Johnson
Robert Parker
Robert Roy
Robert L. Thompson
Roderick Ashley
Roza Malekzadeh
Rudy Tandjono
Sabina M. Poole
Sally Raulerson
Samuel Sauter
Sandi Bruce
Sara Carson-Mohamed
Sarah Norris
Scott Thayer
Serena L. DiPilato
Serge Khoudessian
Seth R. Bradshaw
Shannon Brown
Spencer M. Russell
Staci Pfau
Stacy Swain
Stacy Taylor
Stefee S. Knudsen
Stella Chan
Stephen Korbich
Steven Karolyi
Susan Coulter
Susan Frost
Susan A. Hargrave
Susan M. Lyon
Thomas Cole
Thomas A. Douville
Thomas Ellicott
Thomas Gregg
Thomas G. Motsiff
Thomas Shaw
Tiffonie M. Carroll
Timothy G. Cooke
Timothy Simpson
Timothy P. Wybenga
Tobin Weaver
Tony Burke
Tony Martinez
Tracy Nichols
Tricia R. Dickson
Veronica McCauley
Vijay Deodhar
Wayne Kelly
Whitney D. Allred
William McGee
William Worthington
Yani Vaivoda
Yeda Auten Arscott
Zach Emmingham
Zachary A. Pennell

*Current and past principals are denoted in red

AWARDS & CONTRIBUTIONS

2020
Murphy Headquarters Eugene, Oregon
Finalist, DJC Top Projects—Office: New Construction

2019
Lecture Architecture Foundation of Oregon, Portland, Oregon, 'Park Avenue Perspective'
Visiting Studio Critic University of Oregon College of Design, Eugene, Oregon

2018
Banfield Corporate Headquarters Vancouver, Washington
Honor Award, ACEC Oregon

2017
Park Avenue West Tower Portland, Oregon
Finalist, DJC Top Projects—Mixed-Use
Banfield Corporate Headquarters Vancouver, Washington
First Place, DJC Top Projects—Private

2016
Park Avenue West Tower Portland, Oregon
AIA Portland Mayor's Award for Design Excellence
Park Avenue West Tower Portland, Oregon
Craftsmanship Award, AIA
Visiting Studio Critic University of Oregon College of Design, Eugene, Oregon
Lecture Town Club of Portland, Portland, Oregon, 'The Architecture of Robert Thompson'
Lecture College of Architecture & Urban Design, Tongji University, Shanghai, China, 'Design Process: Nike Greater China Headquarters'

2014
Lecture Nike, Inc., Shanghai, China, 'The Coming of Nike: Greater China Corporate Headquarters'
Visiting Studio Critic University of Washington Department of Architecture, Seattle, Washington, 'Designing in China'

2012
PeaceHealth Corporate Headquarters Vancouver, Washington
Finalist, DJC Top Projects—Renovation
Lecture Architecture Foundation of Oregon, Portland, Oregon, 'Honored Citizen Presentation: Phil and Penny Knight'

2011
Lecture University of Oregon, Eugene, Oregon, 'Design: The Ford Alumni Center' Cambridge Architectural
Lecture University of Oregon College of Design, Portland, Oregon, 'The Design Process: Matthew Knight Arena'
Featured Speaker Robert Thompson, Portland Creative Conference, Portland, Oregon, 'The Design work of TVA Architects. 1984–2011'
Lecture SCI-ARC, Los Angeles, California, 'Innovation in Retail Branding'
Lecture University of Oregon, Eugene, Oregon, 'Matthew Knight Arena + Ford Alumni Center: A Dialogue'

2009
EVO Tower Los Angeles, California
Design Excellence Award, MHN
Green Building of America Award, Real Estate & Construction Review

2008
Nike World Headquarters Beaverton, Oregon
Number 8 of America's Top 100 Sports Venues; ESPN Award
EVO Tower Los Angeles, California
National Geographic Channel: 'LA Hard Hats' Six-part Documentary Special

2007
Lecture Portland Business Alliance, Park Avenue West Tower, Portland, Oregon, 'A Conversation with Robert Thompson'
Wilson Aquatic Pool Renovation Portland, Oregon
Design Award of Excellence, Oregon Recreation & Parks Association

2006
Social Security Administration Building (GSA Call Center) Auburn, Washington
Honor Award for Design Excellence, National GSA

2005
Quantec, LLC Portland, Oregon
Design Award for Sustainable Workplace Design, Portland Office of Sustainable Development

2003
Nike World Headquarters—North Campus Expansion Beaverton, Oregon
Honor Award for Design Excellence, AIA Northwest & Pacific Region
Ericsson North American Headquarters Plano, Texas
Honor Award, IIDA/AIA Interior Design
Honor Award, ASLA

2002
Lecture Procter & Gamble Headquarters, Cincinnati, Ohio, 'Innovation in Workplace Design'
Lecture Washington State University School of Architecture, Pullman, Washington, 'The Architecture of TVA Architects, Inc.'

2000
Nike World Headquarters—North Campus Expansion Beaverton, Oregon
Honor Award for Design Excellence, AIA
Design Award, ASID
Interior Honor Award, ASID
Nike World Headquarters—Mia Hamm Design Center Beaverton, Oregon
Design Award of Excellence, Portland AIA
Honor Award for Design Excellence, IIDA
Merit Award for Design Excellence, IIDA

1999
East Portland Community Center Portland, Oregon
Best Facility Award, Oregon Parks & Recreation
City Center 12 Vancouver Cinemas Vancouver, Washington
Community Design Award
National Steinbeck Museum Salinas, California
Honor Award for Design Excellence, Monterey Bay CA Chapter AIA

1998
East Portland Community Center Portland, Oregon
Governor's Livability Award of Design Excellence, State of Oregon
City Center 12 Vancouver Cinemas Vancouver, Washington
City of Vancouver Planning and Urban Renewal Design Award

1997
Lincoln City Cinemas Lincoln City, Oregon
Merit Design Award—Unbuilt Category, AIA
Juror National AIA Honor Awards Program, AIA, Washington, D.C.
Jurors Malcolm Holzman, Dana Cuff, Joan Goody, Susan Henshaw, Robert Thompson, Robert Yudell, Anne Tyng, Michael Ayles, Aaron Johnson
Juror AIA Design Awards, Spokane Washington Chapter, AIA
Nike World Headquarters—North Campus Walker Entry Guardhouse Beaverton, Oregon
Design Award of Excellence—Unbuilt Category, AIA
Welcome Center at The Grotto Portland, Oregon
Honor Award for Design Excellence, AIA Northwest & Pacific Region
Wilsonville High School Wilsonville, Oregon
Award of Merit for Design Excellence, AIA Northwest & Pacific Region

1996
Welcome Center at The Grotto Portland, Oregon
Honorable Mention, Design Award of Excellence—Unbuilt Projects, AIA Portland
Metro Regional Headquarters Portland, Oregon
Architecture + Energy Award, AIA

1995
Metro Regional Headquarters Portland, Oregon
Honor Award for Design Excellence, AIA Northwest & Pacific Region
Wilsonville High School Wilsonville, Oregon
Design Award of Excellence, AIA

1994
Evergreen Air Venture Museum McMinnville, Oregon
Design Award of Excellence—Unbuilt Category, AIA
Nike Conference Center Beaverton, Oregon
Design Award of Excellence—Unbuilt Category, AIA
Lecture City Club of Portland, Portland, Oregon, 'Portland Architecture: Design and Community,' Robert Thompson, Robert Frasca, and Thomas Hacker
Juror AIA Design Awards Program, Michigan Chapter, AIA

1993
Metro Regional Headquarters Portland, Oregon
Honor Award for Design Excellence, AIA
Nike World Headquarters Beaverton, Oregon
International BOMA-Corporate Campus of the Year

1992
Moyer Meditation Chapel Portland, Oregon
ACEC Honor Award, Engineering Excellence Awards
Moyer Meditation Chapel Portland, Oregon
Tucker Award of Design Excellence, The Building Stone Institute
Bo Jackson Sports & Fitness Center Beaverton, Oregon
People's Choice Award, AIA
Nike World Headquarters Beaverton, Oregon
Portland BOMA-Corporate Campus of the Year
Juror AIA Nebraska Design Awards Program, Robert Frasca, Robert L. Thompson, and Jim Jonassen
Lecture University of Nebraska, Lincoln, Nebraska, 'The Architecture of Thompson Vaivoda & Associates'
Lecture University of Oregon College of Design, Eugene, Oregon, 'Nike World Headquarters'

1991
Nike World Headquarters Beaverton, Oregon
Corporate America Design Award of Excellence, *Interior* magazine
Nike World Headquarters Beaverton, Oregon
Honor Award, AIA Northwest and Pacific Region
Moyer Meditation Chapel Portland, Oregon
Citation Award for New Construction, Interfaith Forum on Religion, Art and Architecture
Moyer Meditation Chapel Portland, Oregon
First Award, People's Choice, AIA
Craftsmanship Award, AIA
Moyer Meditation Chapel Portland, Oregon
Excellence in Concrete Award

1990
Nike World Headquarters Beaverton, Oregon
People's Choice Award, AIA
Craftsmanship Award, AIA
Merit Design Award of Excellence, AIA

1989
Moyer Meditation Chapel Portland, Oregon
Design Award for Unbuilt Projects, AIA
Visiting Studio Critic University of Oregon College of Design, Eugene, Oregon, 'High-Rise Architecture'
Crossroads Cinema Bellevue, Washington
Design Award of Excellence for Lighting/Details, AIA
Nike World Headquarters—Nike Bridges Beaverton, Oregon
Design Award for Unbuilt Projects, AIA

1988
Alden/Drummond Residence Portland, Oregon
Honor Award for Design Excellence, AIA
Craftsmanship Award, AIA
People's Choice Award, AIA

1988
Kaady Car Wash Portland, Oregon
Design Award of Excellence, AIA
Tigard Cinema Tigard, Oregon
Design Award of Excellence, AIA

1987
Lakepoint Center Boise, Idaho
Honor Award for Design Excellence, AIA
Tigard Cinemas Tigard, Oregon
People's Choice Award, AIA
Lecture Portland Chapter, AIA, Portland, Oregon, 'The Art of Design Competitions'

1985
Southtech Business Center Tualatin, Oregon
Commendation Award of Excellence, AIA

1984
Kruse Way Plaza Lake Oswego, Oregon
Honor Award for Design Excellence, AIA
Park Avenue Athletic Club Portland, Oregon
Award for Design Excellence, AIA

1982
Fisher Residence Portland, Oregon
Honor Award for Design Excellence, AIA

1981
Thompson Residence Portland, Oregon
Merit Award for Design Excellence, AIA

PROJECT CREDITS

ALDEN/DRUMMOND RESIDENCE
Client: Jeffery Alden & Donna Drummond
Contractor: Cascade Construction Company
Architect: TVA Architects, Inc.
Design Principal: Robert L. Thompson, FAIA
Project Team: Allan Norris
Mechanical / Electrical / Plumbing: Design/Build
Structural: VanDomelen Looijenga McGarrigle Knauf
Photography: Strode Photographic

ALDER 9 APARTMENTS
Client: VWR Development Co.
Architect: TVA Architects, Inc.
Design Principal: Robert L. Thompson, FAIA
Project Team: Kelly C. Cady, Aaron B. Cook, John M. Jamiel, Eric A. Li, Iain F. MacKenzie, Richard W. Rapp, Spencer M. Russell, Aaron J. Vanderpool
Structural: KPFF Consulting Engineers, Inc.
Mechanical / Plumbing: Jet Industries
Electrical: Whiskey Hill
Civil: David Evans & Associates
Landscape Architect: Shapiro Didway

THE ANIVA APARTMENTS
Client: Civitas Inc.
Contractor: LGC Pence
Architect: TVA Architects, Inc.
Design Principal: Robert L. Thompson, FAIA
Project Team: Seth R. Bradshaw, Kelly C. Cady, John M. Jamiel, Marc A. Labadie, Iain F. MacKenzie, Marie M. Malone, Richard W. Rapp, Spencer M. Russell
Interior Designer: CWA Interiors
Structural: KPFF Consulting Engineers, Inc.
Landscape Architect: Shapiro Didway
Photography: Sally Painter

ANKENY PLAZA PAVILION
Client: Portland Parks and Recreation
Architect: TVA Architects, Inc.
Design Principal: Robert L. Thompson, FAIA
Project Team: Rena J. Ackley, Michael A. Hahn, Marc A. Labadie, Jared Z. Mayzak, Robert Parker, Jeremy Webber, Nicholas J. Williams
Landscape Architect: Walker Macy
Photography: TVA Architects, Inc.

BANFIELD CORPORATE HEADQUARTERS
Client: Banfield Pet Hospital
Contractor: Skanska USA
Architect: TVA Architects, Inc.
Design Principal: Robert L. Thompson, FAIA
Project Team: Kelly C. Cady, Erik F. Dorsett, Susan A. Hargrave, Eric A. Li, David E. Morris, Elisa M. Rocha, Pamela E. Saftler, Mark D. Williams
Interior Designer: Gensler
Structural: KPFF Consulting Engineers, Inc.
Mechanical / Electrical / Plumbing: Interface Engineering, Inc.
Landscape Architect: PLACE
Photography: Terrence Mahanna / Ryan Gobuty, Christian Columbres

BO JACKSON FITNESS CENTER
Client: Nike, Inc.
Contractor: Koll Construction Company, Inc.
Architect: TVA Architects, Inc.
Design Principal: Robert L. Thompson, FAIA
Project Manager: Gregory Miller
Project Team: Marc A. Labadie, Gregory S. Mitchell, Tracy Nichols, Allan Norris
Owner's Design Representative: Howard S. Slusher
Mechanical / Electrical / Plumbing: Interface Engineering, Inc.
Structural: KPFF Consulting Engineers, Inc.
Civil: Waker Associates, Inc.
Landscape Architect: Otak, Inc.
Photography: Strode Photographic, Richard Barnes, Jeff Goldberg / ESTO

THE CARING CABIN
Client: Children's Cancer Association
Contractor: Sunco
Architect: TVA Architects, Inc.
Design Principal: Robert L. Thompson, FAIA
Project Team: Thomas A. Douville, John Heili, Marc A. Labadie, Nicholas J. Williams
Photography: Stephen Cridland, Richard Strode

COACHES OFFICE MKA
Client: University of Oregon
Contractor: Fortis Construction Company
Architect: TVA Architects, Inc.
Design Principal: Robert L. Thompson, FAIA
Project Manager: John M. Jamiel
Project Team: Kelly C. Cady, Erick F. Dorsett, Richard W. Rapp
Branding: Downstream
Interior Designer: CWA Interiors
Structural: KPFF Consulting Engineers, Inc.
Photography: Christian Columbres

CRABBE RESIDENCE
Client: James Crabbe
Contractor: Green Gables
Architect: TVA Architects, Inc.
Design Principal: Robert L. Thompson, FAIA
Project Team: Montgomery J. Hill
Interior Designer: Jill Bayles
Photography: Greg Kozawa / Russ Widstrand / TVA Architects, Inc. / Richard Strode

DIRECTOR PARK PAVILIONS
Client: TMT Development Co. Inc.
Contractor: Hoffman Construction Co.
Architect: TVA Architects, Inc.
Design Principal: Robert L. Thompson, FAIA
Project Team: Daniel B. Bradbury, Aaron Hall, Michael A. Hahn, Colin Hedrick, John Heili, Marc A. Labadie, Caleb Mitchell, Matthew D. Riordan, Peter G. Wilmarth
Structural: KPFF Structural Engineers, Inc.
Landscape Architect: Laurie Olin, OLIN and Mayer/Reed
Photography: Richard Strode

EVO TOWER
Client: Gerding Edlen/ Williams & Dame
Contractor: Howard S. Wright
Architect: TVA Architects, Inc. / GBD Architects
Design Principal: Robert L. Thompson, FAIA
TVA Project Team: Daniel B. Bradbury, Clint E. Cook, Timothy G. Cooke, Thomas A. Douville, Michael A. Hahn, Aaron Hall, John Heili, Nicholas P. Hemmer, Nicole Hipp, Robert A. Johnson, Roza Malekzadeh, Marc A. Labadie, Courtney Miller, Morgan Pintarich, Elisa M. Rocha, Laura M. Sinsel, Peter G. Wilmarth, Nicholas J. Williams, Timothy P. Wybenga
Interior Designer: TVA Architects / GBD Architects
Structural: KPFF Structural Engineers, Inc.
Photography: Craig Dugan / Lawrence Anderson

FORD ALUMNI CENTER
Client: University of Oregon
Contractor: Fortis Construction Co.
Building Architect: TVA Architects, Inc.
Design Principal: Robert L. Thompson, FAIA
Project Team: Daniel B. Bradbury, Kelly C. Cady, Susan A. Hargrave, Marc A. Labadie, Eric A. Li, Michelle M. Lum, Caleb Mitchell
Interior Designer: Opsis Architecture
Structural: Haris Engineers
Mechanical / Electrical / Plumbing: Interface Engineering, Inc.
Landscape Architect: Walker Macy
Photography: Lawrence Anderson / Terrance Manhanna

FORT DALLES TRAINING CENTER
Client: Oregon Military Department + Columbia Gorge Community College
Contractor: Hoffman Construction Company
Architect: TVA Architects, Inc.
Design Principal: Robert L. Thompson, FAIA
Project Team: Aung Barteaux, Kelly C. Cady, Erik F. Dorsett, John J. Gonzales, Marc A. Labadie, David E. Morris, Elisa M. Rocha, Pamela E. Saftler
Interior Designer: CWA Interiors
Structural: KPFF Consulting Engineers, Inc.
Mechanical / Electrical / Plumbing: Glumac International, Inc.
Landscape Architect: Walker Macy
Photography: Terrance Mahanna

FOX TOWER
Client: TMT Development, Inc.
Contractor: Hoffman Construction Company
Architect: TVA Architects, Inc.
Design Principal: Robert L. Thompson, FAIA
Project Managers: Nathan C. Corser, Andre DeBar, AIA
Construction Managers: Gregory S. Mitchell, Eric A. Li
Project Team: Michael Feinstein, Daniel Gero, Robert Hager, Calvert Helms, Brian Higgins, Robert A. Johnson, Renee Kludas, Stephen Korbich, Marc A. Labadie, Eric A. Li, Allan Norris, Sally Raulerson, Chuck Salvador, Samuel Sauter, Darren Schroeder, Timothy Simpson, Noel Snodgrass, Amarjit Singh Tamber, John Thomas, Jerry Waters
Mechanical / Electrical / Plumbing: Glumac International, Inc.
Structural / Civil: KPFF Consulting Engineers, Inc.
Landscape Architect: Mayer/Reed
Interior Designer: Williamson McCarter & Associates
Traffic: Kittelson & Associates
Parking: International Parking Design
Geotechnical: Geotechnical Resources, Inc.
Acoustical: CS Acoustical Engineer
Photography: Strode Photographic

FRANKEL RESIDENCE
Client: Marc & Tracy Frankel
Architect: TVA Architects, Inc.
Design Principals: Robert L. Thompson, FAIA, Roderick Ashley, FAIA
Interior Designer: Robert L. Thompson, FAIA, Roderick Ashley, FAIA
Photography: Stephen Cridland

FRITZ RESIDENCE
Client: Mike and Kristin Fritz
Contractor: Jeffery Hill
Architect: TVA Architects, Inc.
Design Principal: Robert L. Thompson, FAIA
Project Team: Kelly C. Cady, Brian M. Grosklos, Joseph K. Morgan
Interior Designer: CWA Interiors
Structural: Froelich
Landscape Architect: Shapiro Didway
Photography: Christian Columbres

PROJECT CREDITS

GOOSE HOLLOW LOFTS
Client: VWR Development
Contractor: VWR Development
Architect: TVA Architects, Inc.
Design Principal: Robert L. Thompson, FAIA
Project Team: Seth R. Bradshaw, Tiffonie M. Carroll, Paul Darmofal, Elizabeth N. Delorme, Erik F. Dorsett, John M. Jamiel, Marc A. Labadie, Iain F. MacKenzie, Marie M. Malone, Richard W. Rapp, Jeremy Spurgin
Interior Designer: CWA Interiors
Structural: Catena
Mechanical / Electrical / Plumbing: Jet
Landscape Architect: Shapiro Didway
Photography: Terrence Mahanna / Sally Painter

GREVE RESIDENCE
Client: Spencer Greve
Contractor: Ostmo Construction Co.
Architect: TVA Architects, Inc.
Design Principal: Robert L. Thompson, FAIA
Project Team: Kelly C. Cady, John M. Jamiel, Alan Norris, Richard W. Rapp
Interior Designer: CWA Interiors
Structural: Froelich
Landscape Architect: Shapiro Didway
Photography: Christian Columbres

GSA / SSA CALL CENTER
Client: General Services Administration
Contractor: Absher Construction Co.
Architect: TVA Architects, Inc.
Design Principal: Robert L. Thompson, FAIA
Project Team: David P. Gellos, Robert A. Johnson, Marc A. Labadie
Interior Designer: IA Interior Architect
Structural: KPFF Consulting Engineers, Inc.
Mechanical / Electrical / Plumbing: Glumac International, Inc.
Photography: Stephen Cridland / Richard Strode

JERRY RICE BUILDING
Owner: Nike, Inc.
Contractor: Kiewit Construction Co.
Architect: TVA Architects, Inc.
Design Principal: Robert L. Thompson, FAIA
Project Manager: Montgomery J. Hill
Project Team: Andre Debar, Robert A. Johnson, Marc A. Labadie, Allan Norris, Richard W. Rapp
Interior Designer: CWA Interiors
Structural: KPFF Consulting Engineers, Inc.
Mechanical / Electrical / Plumbing: Glumac International, Inc.
Landscape Architect: Mayer Reed
Photography: Strode Photographic

JOHN ROSS TOWER
Client: Block 35 Investors LLC
Contractor: Hoffman Construction Co.
Architect: TVA Architects, Inc. / GBD Architects Joint Venture
Design Principal: Robert L. Thompson, FAIA
Project Team: Daniel B. Bradbury, Clint E. Cook, John Heili, Nicholas P. Hemmer, Montgomery J. Hill, Robert A. Johnson, Marc A. Labadie, Courtney Miller, Morgan Pintarich, Timothy Simpson, Laura M. Sinsel, Mark D. Williams
Interior Designer: CWA Interiors / TVA / GBD
Structural: KPFF Consulting Engineers, Inc.
Mechanical / Electrical / Plumbing: Glumac International, Inc.
Landscape Architect: Murase
Photography: Russ Widstrand / Richard Strode / Christian Columbres

MATTHEW KNIGHT ARENA
Client: University of Oregon
Contractor: Hoffman Construction
Design Architect: TVA Architects, Inc.
Executive Architect: AECOM
Design Principal: Robert L. Thompson, FAIA
TVA Project Team: Param Bedi, Daniel B. Bradbury, Kelly C. Cady, Clint E. Cook, Timothy G. Cooke, Jesse Figgins, Michael A. Hahn, Marc A. Labadie, Caleb Mitchell, Matt Piccone, Robert Parker, Joshua Powell, Mark D. Williams, Peter Wilmarth
Interior Designer: TVA Architects, Inc., AECOM, Perkins & Will
Structural: Haris Engineers
Mechanical / Electrical / Plumbing: Herderson
Civil: Balzhiser Hubbard
Landscape Architect: Walker Macy
Photography: Lawrence Anderson / Terrance Mahanna

METRO HEADQUARTERS
Client: Metro
Contractor: Hoffman Construction Company, Inc.
Architect: TVA Architects, Inc.
Design Principal: Robert L. Thompson, FAIA
Project Principal: Thomas Cole, AIA
Project Manager: Paul Thimm, AIA
Project Team: Gordan Gillan, James Henry, John Medvec, Allan Norris, Kurt K. Schultz
Electrical / Plumbing: Glumac International, Inc.
Structural / Civil: KPFF Consulting Engineers, Inc.
Landscape Architect: Mayer/Reed, Inc.
Interior Designer: Williamson McCarter Associates
Lighting: Glumac International, Inc.
Kitchen: Halliday Associates
Photography: Strode Photographic

MIA HAMM DESIGN CENTER
Client: Nike, Inc.
Contractor: Kiewit Construction Co,
Architect: TVA Architects, Inc.
Design Principal: Robert L. Thompson, FAIA
Project Manager: Leslie Cliffe
Project Team: Tony Burke, Francis Dardis, Marc A. Labadie, Jeffrey Law, Eric A. Li, Richard W. Rapp, Pamela E. Saftler, Chuck Salvador, Thomas Shaw
Structural: KPFF Consulting Engineers, Inc.
Mechanical / Electrical / Plumbing: Glumac International, Inc.
Landscape Architect: Mayer Reed
Interior Designer: CWA Interiors
Signage: Ambrosini Design
Photography: Strode Photographic

PROJECT CREDITS

MOYER MAUSOLEUM
Client: Tom Moyer
Contractor: Precision Co.
Architect: TVA Architects, Inc.
Design Principal: Robert L. Thompson, FAIA
Project Team: Kelly C. Cady, John M. Jamiel
Landscape Architect: TVA Architects, Inc.
Photography: TVA Architects, Inc.

MURPHY CORPORATE OFFICES
Client: Murphy Company
Contractor: Dorman Construction Co.
Architect: TVA Architects, Inc.
Design Principal: Robert L. Thompson, FAIA
Project Manager: John M. Jamiel
Project Team: Kelly C. Cady, Erik F. Dorsett, Richard W. Rapp
Interior Designer: CWA Interiors
Structural: KPFF Consulting Engineers, Inc.
Mechanical / Electrical / Plumbing: Interface Engineering, Inc.
Landscape Architect: Shapiro Didway
Photography: Christian Columbres

NIKE AIR HANGAR
Client: Nike, Inc.
Contractor: Hoffman Construction
Architect: TVA Architects, Inc.
Design Principal: Robert L. Thompson, FAIA
Project Team: Eric A. Li, Montgomery J. Hill, Marc A. Labadie, Pamela E. Saftler
Interior Designer: CWA Interiors
Structural: KPFF Consulting Engineers, Inc.
Mechanical / Electrical / Plumbing: PAE
Landscape Architect: Shapiro Didway
Photography: Stephen Cridland / Richard Strode

NIKE ASIAN CORPORATE HEADQUARTERS
Client: Nike, Inc.
Developer: Tishman Speyer
Architect: TVA Architects, Inc.
Design Principal: Robert L. Thompson, FAIA
Project Team: Daniel B. Bradbury, Kelly C. Cady, Dimitri C. Englert, Marc A. Labadie, Philip Krueger, Zachary A. Pennell, Jonas Rake, Mark D. Williams
Interior Designer: CWA Interiors
Mechanical / Electrical / Plumbing: Glumac International, Inc.
Photography: Frans Wang

NIKE GATEHOUSE
Owner: Nike, Inc.
Contractor: Kiewit Construction Co.
Architect: TVA Architects, Inc.
Design Principal: Robert L. Thompson, FAIA
Project Team: Marc A. Labadie, Allan Norris, Richard W. Rapp
Structural: KPFF Consulting Engineers, Inc.
Mechanical / Electrical / Plumbing: Glumac International, Inc.
Landscape Architect: Robert Murase
Photography: Strode Photographic

NIKE RETAIL STORES—ATLANTA
Client: Nike, Inc.
Contractor: David Nice Builders
Architect: TVA Architects, Inc.
Principal: Robert L. Thompson, FAIA
Project Manager: John Heili
Project Team: Aung Barteaux, Daniel B. Bradbury, Erik F. Dorsett, Marc A. Labadie, Philip Krueger, Elisa M. Rocha, Nicholas J. Williams
Interior Designer: Richard Clarke, Nike Creative Director; Keith Wilkins, Nike Design Director; Ryan Lingard, Nike Senior Designer;
Structural: KPFF Consulting Engineers, Inc.
Mechanical / Electrical / Plumbing: KLH Engineers
Photography: Michael Wells

NIKE RETAIL STORES—CHICAGO
Client: Nike, Inc.
Contractor: Crane Construction Co.
Architect: TVA Architects, Inc.
Principal: Robert L. Thompson, FAIA
Project Manager: John Heili
Project Team: Aung Barteaux, Erik F. Dorsett, Marc A. Labadie, Pearse D. O'Moore, Jonas Rake, Nicholas J. Williams
Interior Designer: Richard Clarke, Nike Creative Director; Luis Rueda, Nike Design Director; Ryan Lingard, Nike Senior Designer; Brad Berman, Senior Project Director and Owners Representative
Structural: KPFF Consulting Engineers, Inc.
Mechanical / Electrical / Plumbing: KLH Engineers
Photography: Mo Daoud

NIKE RETAIL STORES—SANTA MONICA
Client: Nike, Inc.
Contractor: Macerich
Architect: TVA Architects, Inc.
Design Principal: Robert L. Thompson, FAIA
Project Team: Kelly C. Cady, John Heili, Montgomery J. Hill, Eric A. Li
Interior Designer: Howard Lichter, Nike Creative Director; Tim Perks, Nike Design Director; Brad Berman, Senior Project Director and Owners Representative
Structural: KPFF Consulting Engineers, Inc.
Mechanical / Electrical / Plumbing: Glumac International, Inc.
Photography: Charles Chestnut / Lawrence Anderson

NIKE RETAIL STORES—SEATTLE
Client: Nike, Inc.
Architect: TVA Architects, Inc.
Principal: Robert L. Thompson, FAIA
Project Team: Tiffonie Carroll, John Heili, Pearse D. O'Moore, Elisa M. Rocha, Pamela E. Saftler
Interior Designer: Nike Retail Design
Structural: KPFF Consulting Engineers, Inc.
Mechanical / Electrical / Plumbing: KLH Engineers
Photography: Michael Wells

PROJECT CREDITS

NIKE SPORTS PERFORMANCE CENTER

Client: Nike, Inc.

Contractor: Hoffman Construction Co.

Architect: TVA Architects, Inc.

Design Principal: Robert L. Thompson, FAIA

Project Team: Joann Hermance, Montgomery J. Hill, Mark A. Labadie

Interior Designer: CWA Interiors

Structural: KPFF Consulting Engineers, Inc.

Mechanical / Electrical / Plumbing: Glumac International, Inc.

Landscape Architect: Mayer Reed

Photography: Strode Photographic

NIKE WORLD HEADQUARTERS

Client: Nike, Inc.

Contractor: Koll Construction Company, Inc.

Architect: TVA Architects, Inc.

Design Principal: Robert L. Thompson, FAIA

Project Managers: David P. Gellos, AIA, Marc A. Labadie, Gregory Miller

Project Team: Mark Annen, Thomas Ellicott, Andrew Feinberg, Eric Gamer, Daniel Gates, Kevin Gernhardt, Gordon Gillan, Thomas Gregg, Bruce Kenny, John Medvec, Gregory S. Mitchell, Carolyn Murray, Tracy Nichols, Allan Norris, Robert Roy, Kurt K. Schultz, Thomas Shaw, James Smith, Paul Smith

Owner's Design Representative: Howard S. Slusher

Mechanical / Electrical / Plumbing: Interface Engineering, Inc.

Civil: Waker Associates, Inc.

Landscape Architect: Otak, Inc., Murase Associates

Interior Architect—Offices: Wyatt Stapper Architects

Interior Architect—Public Spaces: Thompson Vaivoda & Associates, Inc.

Signage: Ambrosini Design Ltd.

Kitchen: Halliday Associates

Photography: Strode Photographic, Jeff Goldberg / ESTO, Richard Barnes

NIKE WORLD HEADQUARTERS— NORTH EXPANSION

Client: Nike, Inc.

Contractor: Kiewit Construction Company, Inc. Hoffman Construction Company

Architect: TVA Architects, Inc.

Design Principal: Robert L. Thompson, FAIA

Overall Project Managers: Clark Brockamn, Marc A. Labadie,

Project Managers: Leslie Cliffe, Gordon Gillan, Joann Hermance, AIA, Montgomery J. Hill, Richard W. Rapp, Pamela E. Saftler, Rudy Tandjono

Site Managers: Arthur Asgian, Wayne Kelly

Project Team: Andrzej Babiracki, Jeffrey Bromwell, Tony Burke, Raymond Cheng, Clint E. Cook, Brien Costello, Susan Coulter, Neil Cristal, Francis Dardis, Andre DeBar, AIA, Vijay Deodhar, Thomas A. Douville, Michael Feinstein, Alan Gerencer, Daniel Gero, Robert Hager, John Heili, Robert Ilosvay, Janet Foz Jacobs, Robert A. Johnson, Steven Karolyi, Alexander Khesin, Renee Kludas, Stephen Korbich, Jeffrey law, Eric A. Li, Veronica McCauley, Daniel McFarland, Gregory S. Mitchell, Alan Norris, Michael Payne, Richard W. Rapp, Sally Raulerson, Chuck Salvador, Darren Schroeder, Thomas Shaw, Timothy Simpson, John Thomas, Jerry Waters, Tobin Weaver, Peter G. Wilmarth, Craig Witte, Johannes Zech

Owner's Design Representative: Howard S. Slusher

Mechanical / Electrical / Plumbing: Glumac International, Inc., PAE Consulting Engineers

Structural: KPFF Consulting Engineers, Inc., Cary Kopczynski, Inc.

Civil: W&H Pacific, Inc.

Geotechnical: AGRA Environmental, Inc.

Landscape Architect: Mayer/Reed, Murase Associates, Rich Haag Associates

Interior Designer: Williamson McCarter & Associates

Signage: Ambrosini Design Ltd.

Acoustical: McKay Conant Brook, Inc.

Kitchen: Halliday Associates

Photography: Strode Photographic

NOLAN RYAN BUILDING

Client: Nike, Inc.

Contractor: Kiewit Construction Company, Inc.

Architect: TVA Architects, Inc.

Design Principal: Robert L. Thompson, FAIA

Project Manager: Marc A. Labadie

Project Team: Andrew Feinberg, Daniel Gates, David P. Gellos, Gordan Gillan, James Henry, William McGee, Gregory Miller, Gregory S. Mitchell, Tracy Nichols, Allan Norris, Robert Roy, James Smith, Kurt K. Schultz, Randy Williams

Owner's Design Representative: Howard S. Slusher

Mechanical / Electrical / Plumbing: Glumac International, Inc.

Structural: KPFF Consulting Engineers, Inc.

Civil: Waker Associates, Inc.

Landscape Architect: Otak, Inc., Murase Associates

Lighting: Glumac International, Inc.

Photography: Strode Photographic

OCHOCO AIR HANGAR

Client: Nike, Inc.

Contractor: Hoffman Construction

Architect: TVA Architects, Inc.

Design Principal: Robert L. Thompson, FAIA

Project Team: Kelly C. Cady, John J. Gonzales, Susan A. Hargrave, Marc A. Labadie, Eric A. Li, David E. Morris, Pamela E. Saftler

Interior Designer: CWA Interiors

Structural: KPFF Consulting Engineers, Inc.

Mechanical / Electrical / Plumbing: Glumac International, Inc.

Landscape Architect: PLACE

Photography: Charles Chestnut, Terrence Mahanna

PROJECT CREDITS

THE PARK
Owner: Nike, Inc.
Contractor: Howard S. Wright
Architect: TVA Architects, Inc.
Design Principal: Robert L. Thompson, FAIA
Project Team: Marc A. Labadie, Peter G. Wilmarth, Craig Witte
Structural: Cary Kopczynski
Mechanical / Electrical / Plumbing: Glumac International, Inc.
Photography: Strode Photographic

PARK AVENUE WEST TOWER
Client: TMT Development Company
Contractor: Hoffman Construction Co.
Architect: TVA Architects, Inc.
Design Principal: Robert L. Thompson, FAIA
Project Manager: Elisa M. Rocha, Mark D. Williams
Project Team: Alexandre X. Asselineau, Daniel B. Bradbury, Kelly C. Cady, Daniel L. Childs, John J. Gonzales, John T. Heinen, John M. Jamiel, Philip Kreuger, Marc A. Labadie, Zachary A. Pennell
Interior Designer: CWA Interiors
Structural: KPFF Consulting Engineers, Inc.
Mechanical / Electrical / Plumbing: Interface Engineering, Inc.
Landscape Architect: Mayer/Reed
Photography: Lawrence Anderson / Terrence Mahanna / Christian Columbres

PEARL APARTMENTS
Client: Paul Properties / Johnson 13, LLC / Andrew Paul
Contractor: Seabold Construction
Architect: TVA Architects, Inc.
Design Principal: Robert L. Thompson, FAIA
Project Team: Kelly C. Cady, Bonnie P. Chiu-Wong, John M. Jamiel, Eric A. Li, Joseph K. Morgan, Richard W. Rapp, Elisa M. Rocha, Spencer M. Russell, Aaron J. Vanderpool
Interior Designer: CWA Interiors
Structural: KPFF Consulting Engineers, Inc.
Mechanical / Electrical / Plumbing: EC Electric
Landscape Architect: Shapiro Didway

SONY ERICSSON HEADQUARTERS
Client: Ericsson Inc.
Contractor: Austin Commercial, Inc.
Architect: TVA Architects, Inc.
Design Principal: Robert L. Thompson FAIA, David P. Gellos, AIA
Project Manager: Tony Burke
Project Architect: Clint E. Cook
Project Team: Darin Dougherty, Amy Fewkes, Gordon Gillan, Susan Hargrave, John Heili, Montgomery J. Hill, Robert A. Johnson, Marc A. Labadie, Veronica McCauley, Daniel McFarland, Allan Norris, Chuck Salvador, Noel Snodgrass, Edward Vaivoda Jr., Craig Witte
Associate Architect: Gideon Toal, Inc.
Mechanical / Electrical / Plumbing: Purdy-McGuire, Inc.
Structural: Gideon Toal, Inc.
Civil: Kimley-Horn
Landscape Architect: MESA Design Group
Interior Work Environment: The Lauck Group
Photography: Strode Eckert Photographic

SOU PERFORMING ARTS CENTER
Client: Southern Oregon University / Jefferson Public Radio
Contractor: Ausland Group
Architect: TVA Architects, Inc.
Design Principal: Robert L. Thompson, FAIA
Principal: Amanda S. Butler
Project Team: Seth R. Bradshaw, Kelly C. Cady, Dimitri C. Englert, John J. Gonzales, Eric A. Li, Pearse D. O'Moore, Marcy E. Pierce, Kathryn A. Seifert
Interior Designer: TVA Architects, Inc.
Structural: ZCS Engineering
Mechanical / Electrical / Plumbing: Glumac International, Inc.
Landscape Architect: KenCairn
Photography: Christian Columbres / Jim Craven

TIGER WOODS CONFERENCE CENTER
Client: Nike, Inc.
Contractor: Hoffman Construction Co.
Architect: TVA Architects, Inc.
Design Principal: Robert L. Thompson, FAIA
Project Team: Michael Feinstein, Marc A. Labadie, Pamela E. Saftler
Interior Designer: CWA Interiors
Structural: KPFF Consulting Engineers, Inc.
Mechanical / Electrical / Plumbing: Glumac International, Inc.
Landscape Architect: Mayer Reed
Photography: Strode Eckert, Charles Chestnut / Terrence Mahanna

VANCOUVER OFFICE TOWER
Client: Gramor Development Co.
Architect: TVA Architects, Inc.
Design Principal: Robert L. Thompson, FAIA
Project Team: Kelly C. Cady, John M. Jamiel

VANCOUVER WATERFRONT CONDOMINIUM TOWER
Architect: TVA Architects, Inc.
Design Principal: Robert L. Thompson, FAIA
Project Team: Kelly C. Cady, John M. Jamiel, Richard W. Rapp

WEST HILLS RESIDENCE
Client: Steven and Sandra Holmes
Contractor: Steven Holmes
Architect: TVA Architects, Inc.
Design Principal: Robert L. Thompson, FAIA
Project Team: Susan A. Hargrave, Marc A. Labadie
Interior Designer: CWA Interiors
Structural: ABHT
Civil: KPFF Consulting Engineers, Inc.
Landscape Architect: Shapiro Didway
Photography: David Papazian / Stephen Cridland

ACKNOWLEDGMENTS

This body of work would not be possible without the tremendous faith and trust of our clients in the creative process, and their commitment to executing our work at the highest level. Their passion, vision, and collaborative participation in the design process have allowed us to collectively pursue solutions that support and enhance their business goals while creating meaningful and impactful architecture.

Architecture is a team effort enlisting the skills and talents of an enormous body of trusted consultants who have contributed to these projects at the highest level sharing their deep knowledge, commitment, and expertise in their respected fields to ensure the success of our work.

I am extremely grateful to my partners both past and present, including Pam Saftler, Tim Wybenga, and Mandy Butler. Over the past 40 years I have been blessed to work with a gifted and exceedingly talented staff of collaborators who have put their heart and soul into the execution of the work included in this monograph. I have always believed that the success of our firm is the direct by-product of this tremendous talent and commitment to excellence and is what has made my journey over the past 40 years as rewarding and fulfilling as it has been.

I want to thank Nike founder Phil Knight and project director Howard Slusher for taking a risk and believing in a young empassioned architect and for their loyalty and friendship over the past 30 years. To Ned Vaivoda, David Gellos, and Rick Tiland, who shared with me the start of our journey together on that wet October morning in 1984 with four drawing tables, rolls of tracing paper, pencils, colored markers along with a wealth of passion, inspiration, and excitement centered on the belief that we could make a difference and together create a significant body of meaningful architecture. To Russ Hansen and David Dunahugh who gave me the runway and a path to fly at the inception of my career and to Tom Moyer who opened the door to a career filled with opportunity and architectural reward.

I want to extend my deepest appreciation to Kelly Cady, Luke Janzen, and Anita Alastra for devoting their time, enormous talent, and commitment to the execution of this monograph.

We collaborated together yet remotely throughout 2021 during the height of the global COVID-19 Pandemic.

I thank you all.

Robert L. Thompson

Published in Australia in 2022 by
The Images Publishing Group Pty Ltd
ABN 89 059 734 431

Offices

Melbourne
6 Bastow Place
Mulgrave, Victoria 3170
Australia
Tel: +61 3 9561 5544

New York
6 West 18th Street 4B
New York City, NY 10011
United States
Tel: +1 212 645 1111

Shanghai
6F, Building C, 838 Guangji Road
Hongkou District, Shanghai 200434
China
Tel: +86 021 31260822

books@imagespublishing.com
www.imagespublishing.com

Copyright © The Images Publishing Group Pty Ltd 2022
The Images Publishing Group Reference Number: 1606

All rights reserved. Apart from any fair dealing for the purposes of private study, research, criticism or review as permitted under the Copyright Act, no part of this publication may be reproduced, stored in a retrieval system or transmitted in any form by any means, electronic, mechanical, photocopying, recording or otherwise, without the written permission of the publisher.

All imagery is supplied courtesy of TVA Architects and all photography is attributed in the Project Credits on pages 456–61, unless otherwise noted. Front cover: Lawrence Anderson (Matthew Knight Arena); back cover: Michael Wells (Nike Retail Stores–Atlanta); pages 2–3: Michael Wells (Nike Retail Stores–Atlanta); page 4: Terrance Mahanna (Matthew Knight Arena); page 5: Craig Dugan / Lawrence Anderson (EVO Tower); page 9 *top left*: Richard Strode (Kruse Way Plaza), *middle left*: Strode Photographic (Mia Hamm Design Center, Nike World Headquarters), *bottom left*: Terrance Mahanna (Matthew Knight Arena), *right*: Lawrence Anderson (Park Avenue West Tower); page 10: Terrance Mahanna (215 NW Park); page 15 *top left*: Strode Photographic (Fox Tower), *top right*: Strode Photographic (Mia Hamm Design Center, Nike World Headquarters), *right*: Frans Wang (Nike Asian Corporate Headquarters); page 263: Jeff Goldberg / ESTO (Bo Jackson Fitness Center, Nike World Headquarters)

 A catalogue record for this book is available from the National Library of Australia

Title: Robert L Thompson: TVA Architects
ISBN: 9781864709131

This title was commissioned in IMAGES' Melbourne office and produced as follows:
Editorial Georgia (Gina) Tsarouhas, Jeanette Wall *Graphic design* Ryan Marshall *Production* Nicole Boehringer

Printed and bound in China by Artron Art Group on 157gsm Chinese OJI matt art paper (FSC®) matt art paper

IMAGES has included on its website a page for special notices in relation to this and its other publications. Please visit www.imagespublishing.com

Every effort has been made to trace the original source of copyright material contained in this book. The publishers would be pleased to hear from copyright holders to rectify any errors or omissions.

The information and illustrations in this publication have been prepared and supplied by TVA Architects. While all reasonable efforts have been made to ensure accuracy, the publishers do not, under any circumstances, accept responsibility for errors, omissions and representations express or implied.

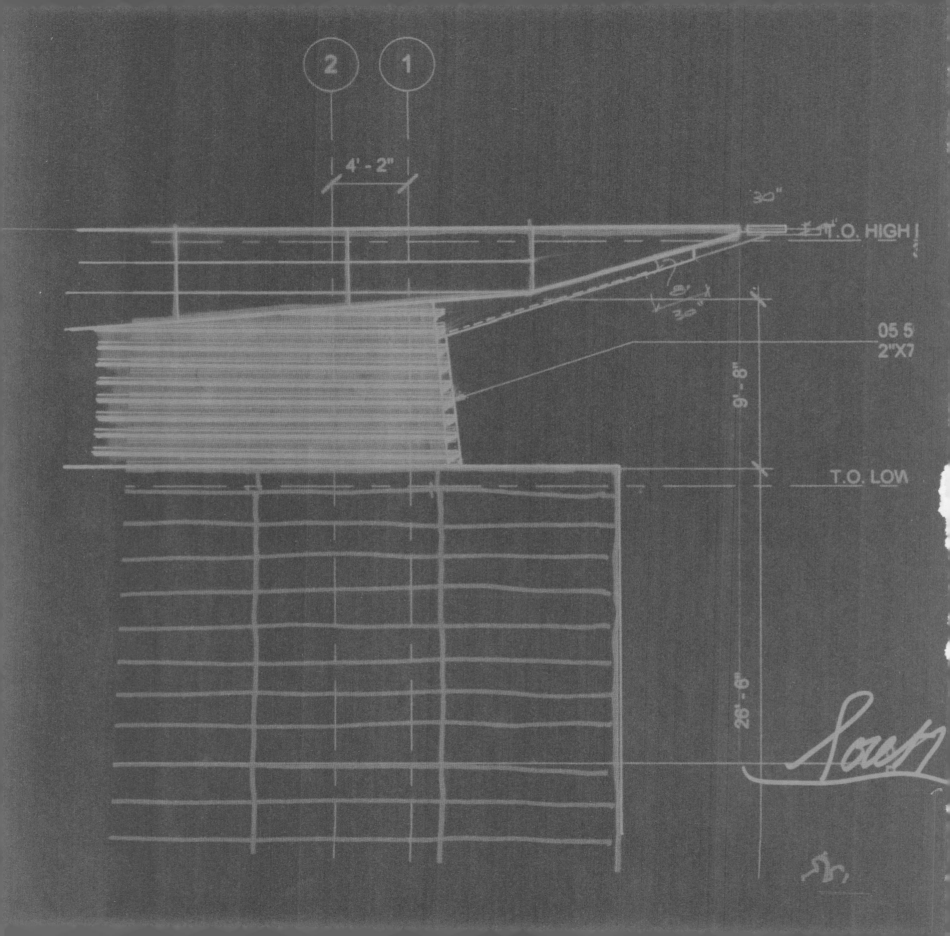